Excel

YEARS 7 to 10

Developing Your Comprehension Skills

ESSENTIAL skills

Get the Results You Want!

PASCAL PRESS

Kristine Brown

Revised edition 2005

Reprinted 2007, 2008, 2009, 2010 (twice), 2011 (twice), 2013, 2014, 2015, 2017, 2019, 2020, 2021, 2022, 2023, 2024

ISBN 978 1 74125 002 2

Pascal Press
PO Box 250
Glebe NSW 2037
(02) 9198 1748
www.pascalpress.com.au

Publisher: Vivienne Joannou
Edited by Emma Hardman and Emma Driver
Cover, design and page layout by DiZign Pty Ltd
Printed by Vivar Printing/Green Giant Press

Contents

Acknowledgments iv

Before you start v

Part One: Key Reading Skills — 1

1	Skimming for gist or preview	3
2	Scanning for specific information	7
3	Predicting	11
4	Working out word meanings	15
5	Understanding writer's purpose and text organisation	18
6	Understanding main ideas	22
7	Understanding detail	27
8	Understanding complex sentences	32
9	Understanding graphs and tables	35
10	Inferring	40
11	Reading critically	45

Part Two: Reading Texts — 51

12	Newsworthiness	*Textbook extract*	52
13	Never say die	*Feature article extract*	56
14	Contact — Part One	*Novel extract*	60
15	Contact — Part Two	*Novel extract*	64
16	Cannibalism in animals	*Fact sheet*	68
17	Pocket money tops $50	*Newspaper report*	72
18	How science began to solve crimes	*Information book extract*	75
19	Life on the edge	*Feature article extract*	78
20	Tapioca to the rescue	*Newspaper report*	82
21	Night of Passage — Part One	*Novel extract*	86
22	Night of Passage — Part Two	*Novel extract*	90
23	Rap music — the beginnings	*Webpage*	94
24	Human cloning	*Letters to the editor*	98
25	Games — Part One	*Novel extract*	101
26	Games — Part Two	*Novel extract*	104
27	Youth smoking drops and mobiles get credit	*Newspaper report*	108
28	Social comment	*Cartoons*	112
29	The Gathering	*Novel extract*	116
30	The Lord of the Rings: The Two Towers	*Film review*	120
31	The International Space Station	*Webpage*	124

Answers 129

Acknowledgements

I would like to thank the following people for their very kind permission to use their materials in this book.

- Tiffany Height and Quantum Market Research for the graphs on pages 36–38.
- Australian Bureau of Statistics for the table on page 39.
- Jackie French and HarperCollins Publishers for the extract from *The Secret Beach* on page 42.
- Allen Baillie and Penguin Books for the extract from *Hero* on page 43.
- Pascal Press for the extract from 'Streetscape', by Ian Steep (from the short story collection *Through the Web and other stories*) on page 41; and for the extract 'Newsworthiness' by John D Fitzgerald (from *Shaping the News*) on page 52.
- Nikki Barrowclough for the extract from 'Never Say Die', *Sydney Morning Herald*, Good Weekend, 12 May 2001, on page 56.
- Penny Hall and HarperCollins Publishers for the two extracts from *Contact*, on pages 60 and 64.
- International Masters Publishers Australia Pty Ltd, for 'Cannibalism', Wildlife Factfile, Card 14, Group 8, Animal Behaviour, on page 68.
- Johanna Leggatt for 'Pocket Money Tops $50', *The Sun-Herald*, 20 October 2002, on page 73.
- Anita Larsen and Scholastic Inc for 'How science began to solve crimes', from *True crimes and how they solved*, on page 77.
- Deidre Macken for the extract from 'Life on the Edge', *Sydney Morning Herald*, Spectrum, 17 January 1998, on page 78.
- Stephanie Peatling for 'Tapioca to the Rescue', *Sydney Morning Herald*, 25 October 2002, on page 82.
- Lee Harding and Penguin Books Australia for the two extracts from 'Night of Passage' (from the short story collection *Dream Time*) on pages 86 and 90.
- Robin Klein and Penguin Books Australia for the two extracts from *Games* on page 101 and page 104.
- Mark Ragg for 'Youth smoking drops and mobiles get credit', *Sydney Morning Herald*, 4/11/00, on page 108.
- Phil Somerville for the two cartoons on page 113.
- Isabelle Carmody and Penguin Books Australia for the extract from *The Gathering* on page 116.
- Will McLean for the drawings used in activities on pages 106 and 118.

I would like to give my special thanks to Hamish McLean for thoroughly trialling the material and for always giving his honest and thoughtful feedback on texts and activities.

Before you start

Which of these students sounds like you?

- Reading is harder in high school. The texts are longer and more complicated.
- I love reading but I don't always understand everything.
- I like reading fiction, but I find reading information texts a bit boring.
- Reading novels is harder for me than reading information texts.
- I can read OK, but I often lose track of what the writer is saying.
- It's hard sometimes to find exactly what I'm looking for when I'm doing research.
- I sometimes have to read things over and over again till I understand them.
- I waste a lot of time looking up the words I don't understand.
- I read a lot but I often skip parts because they look hard.

Perhaps none of them *exactly* describes your thoughts about reading, but probably at least one is close to what you think. Even very skilled and experienced readers sometimes find reading a challenge.

Reading is fun, but it can get harder as you get older and have to read more difficult texts. *Developing Your Comprehension Skills Years 7–10* aims to help you with this.

This book has:

- a wide variety of topics to cover a range of reader interests — youth issues, music, science, current affairs, film, sport, the environment, and the future.
- a mix of fiction and non-fiction.
- activities to develop your reading skills, not just test whether you can get the right answer.
- an answer section to explain the answers and so help you understand even better.
- explanations of the key reading skills so that you can learn how to improve them.

The texts are at a level of difficulty that students from Years 7 to 10 have to deal with every day, and the activities target skills you need to develop for success in these school years. However, everyone is different and it is possible you will find a few texts and activities a little difficult, especially if you are in Year 7, or a little easy, especially if you are in Year 10. If so, it is OK to leave these out, but you should at least give all the activities a quick try first.

The book is divided into two parts. The first part, **Key reading skills**, explains the most important skills you need to read well. It contains activities which will make you more aware of these skills and give you practice in using them.

The second part, **Reading texts**, contains a number of texts, usually a page in length, and activities to help you understand them.

You can work all the way through Part One and then do Part Two. Or, you can go back and forth between the two parts. It is up to you.

I hope you enjoy using the book. I enjoyed writing it for you. I feel confident that you will improve your reading skills by working through it.

So, good luck and happy reading!

Key Reading Skills part 1

Reading involves many different kinds of skills. The good news is that you can develop these skills, and so become a better reader.

When you read, you don't always use the same skills or use them in the same way. This will depend on:

- your purpose in reading a text
- the kind of text you are reading, and
- how easy or difficult the text is.

Your reading purpose

Basically, you read either for pleasure or for information. And the skills you use depend to a large extent on this **general purpose**. But you also usually have a more **specific purpose** for reading. For example, you might be reading a text for just one tiny piece of information — a fact, a word, a number — in answer to a question.

The type of text

The way you read also depends on the **type of text** you are reading. How many of these have you read in the past day or two?

- emails
- text messages
- school notices
- newspaper articles
- plays
- Internet chat
- advertisements
- novels
- webpages of various kinds
- poetry
- cartoons
- bus timetables
- magazine articles
- school notices
- textbooks

For each of these, you probably use your reading skills to a different extent. For example, you probably often have to guess meanings of words when you are reading a novel, but you probably don't need to do this when you are using a bus timetable.

How difficult the text is

Some of the texts you read are much easier than others. If the language used is familiar, you won't have to work so hard to understand the whole text meaning. Or, if you know a lot about a topic or are very interested in it, this will make it easier to read. For example, you might be fascinated by motor bikes and be able to make your way through articles and manuals that most people your age would find impossible.

Some texts are more difficult than others because of how well they are written. Some writers make it easy for the reader. Other writers don't.

Key skills

This part of the book helps you to become more aware of the skills you need to understand what you read. It tells you

- **WHAT** the skills are
- **HOW** to develop and apply the skills, and
- **WHY** you need them.

It also gives you practice in using the key skills. You'll get further practice in using these and other skills in Part Two of the book.

Skimming for gist or preview 1

WHAT?

Skimming is when you run your eyes very quickly over a text to get a general idea of what it is about.

You often do this to preview a text *before* you read it more fully. For example, you might skim the pages of a textbook to decide if it is on the topic you want.

But you also might sometimes skim *instead of* reading a text in a detailed way — when the gist or general idea is enough for your purpose. Most people, for example, skim when they are reading a newspaper or magazine. They don't have the time or interest to read every article in detail.

HOW?

When you skim, you

- look especially at headings, highlighted words and picture captions
- usually read the first paragraph of a text fully and perhaps also the first sentences of each paragraph
- take notice of some words, especially if you seem them again and again
- do *not* read every single word or every detail
- do *not* worry about parts that you do not understand
- keep your eyes moving right through the text; don't get stuck in one section only.

WHY?

You skim to get a general idea about

- the content of a text, e.g. Is it on a topic or theme you are interested in? Will it give you the information you need?
- the purpose of a text, e.g. Is it written to entertain? To inform? To persuade? To explain?
- the kind of writing, e.g. Is it comic or serious? Does it have lots of dialogue? Lots of description?
- the level of difficulty of a text, e.g. Is it dense and academic?

Skimming before you read sets up expectations of what you will meet in the text, and this helps you to read and understand better.

There are many skimming activities in Part Two, mostly in the Preparing to Read sections. Try to stick to any time limits given, to force yourself to skim quickly.

PRACTICE

answers page 129

These skimming activities will show you how much you can understand about a text by skimming *only.*

1 The newspaper articles below are from the 'News in Brief' section of the newspaper. Match the articles to their headlines (underneath) as quickly as you can. **Skim** only. Don't read the whole article.

a A mother who cradled her baby as she was hurled five metres headfirst off a bridge into a waterfall yesterday said she was amazed they escaped alive. The bizarre incident occurred as gale-force winds swept across the northern suburbs for three hours. The mother escaped with only a broken arm and, miraculously, the baby survived the experience without a scratch.

b An unconscious man found wedged between rocks in the Blue Mountains west of Sydney was yesterday winched to safety by rescue crews. The man had been lost for three days in the bush before falling down a steep ravine and becoming pinned between three large boulders. He has head, leg and spinal injuries and is in a critical condition in North Shore hospital.

c Shark sightings forced the closure of three popular South Coast beaches on the weekend. After a number of swimmers reported their fears to the beach patrol, an aerial patrol was called to the area and the presence of five sharks was confirmed. Closures have become a familiar event for swimmers in the area during the summer, although at this stage the reason for the sharks' behaviour is not clear.

d Police have warned businesses in the city's west to be on the lookout for counterfeit \$50 and \$100 notes. More than ten fake notes have been handed in over the past month. Police say it is quite simple to detect that the notes are not real as the graphics are blurred and the writing is larger than on authentic notes. Bars and clubs appear to be the main target but at least two notes were used in shopping complexes.

e A 35-year-old man survived a speedboat accident on the weekend while racing on the Nepean River. The injured man, from the Central Coast, suffered chest and back injuries but was last night in a stable condition in Nepean Hospital. The boat in which he was racing sank and was thought to be beyond repair.

f Police have charged a 24-year-old man from Adelaide with possession of explosive goods after a tip-off from the manager of a local sportsclub. The manager saw a man acting suspiciously in the club car park early yesterday morning, so recorded the car's number plate and rang the police. Police investigating the case said that the explosives were not particularly powerful but commended the manager's quick actions.

Race Smash	Counterfeit Alert	Mountain Fall
Explosives Find	Bridge Miracle	More Beach Closures

2 Give yourself 60 seconds only to skim the text below. After reading, answer the questions without looking back at the text. You will probably be surprised at how much you know. After you finish, check the answers yourself by going back and reading the text fully.

(NOTE: There are more questions about this text in Section 6: Understanding main ideas.)

The Great Kissing Epidemic

paragraph

One theory is that it all began when cavemen began licking their neighbours' **1**
cheeks for the salt on them. But whatever its origins might have been, the fact remains that, in one form or another, kissing has been prevalent since primitive times, though it developed mostly in the West.

Ancient Greek and Roman parents kissed their children, and lovers or married **2**
people kissed each other, as did friends of the same or different sex. In the Middle Ages knights kissed before doing battle, just as boxers touch gloves today before they begin the bout. Relics and images of Christ and the saints were often kissed to express reverence and devotion.

The varieties of kisses are indeed numerous. There is the kiss of treachery (Judas' **3**
kiss is an example of this); the Mafia kiss of death has its own grim significance; the kiss of religious reverence is still a common sight in churches; and there is the kiss 'to-make-it-better', the kiss for luck, the kiss of greeting and the kiss of love.

Kissing is very much a cultural practice and rules and attitudes vary across the **4**
globe. The French, who have had quite a lot of practice, have turned kissing into a fine social art, although these days, even they are not sure when or how to do it. The French double kiss is routine, but many French kiss one another three, or even more, times. It can sometimes go on for an embarrassingly long time. Italians are enthusiastic kissers at all times, and they have been for generations, if not for centuries. Arabic men greet one another with kisses, as do Arabic women. Russian men too are often seen greeting one another with kisses, and it is especially noticeable in the world of Russian politics, where the three-kiss greeting has become the norm. The British, though, remain shy about social kissing. The Japanese, along with many Asian peoples, regard kissing, at least in public, as a Western custom, unhygienic and sometimes even offensive. Kissing has, however, become more commonplace in some Asian countries in the past few decades.

But, despite the resistance of the British, and the opposition of some Eastern **5**
countries, kissing does seem to be on the increase as a social gesture. According to some sociologists, increased kissing is part of a general 'inflation' of intimate social signals. In other words, we kiss people we used to hug, we hug people we used to shake hands with, and we shake hands with those we used to nod to.

a What is one theory of how kissing began?

b Has kissing developed most in Eastern or Western countries?

c What is one example of kissing from past times?

d What is one variety of kissing mentioned?

e Give an example of kissing rules or attitudes in one country.

f Is kissing on the increase or decrease?

Scanning for specific information

2

WHAT?

Scanning is when you look through a text to find **specific information** — perhaps a fact, a name, a statistic, or a quotation.

Scanning is what you do when you look in the phone book for someone's phone number. You are not interested in anything else but that one number.

HOW?

When you scan for specific information, you

- use headings and highlighted words to guide you to the right spot
- move your eyes quickly looking for the information and ignore everything else
- slow down when you get to a part that looks as if it might be what you are looking for, and read it more closely
- don't worry about parts of the text you do not understand.

WHY?

You scan for information because you simply don't need *every* bit of information in *every* text in *every* situation.

You scan because you don't have time to read everything. Imagine how long it would take to find a phone number if you didn't scan the pages to find it, and instead read every name and number.

You mostly use scanning when you are reading for information. This might be scanning the 'For sale' advertisements to find an item you want, or scanning a TV program to find out when a show is on, or scanning to find information to use in an assignment.

There are a number of scanning activities in Part Two. Try to do these by scanning *only* and not by reading the text in full.

PRACTICE

answers page 129

The scanning activities below will show you how effective scanning can be when looking for specific information.

1 Read each question below and then scan the *Program of Events* to find the answer. Do it as quickly as you can. (Note: If asked 'when' questions, give day as well as time.)

a You want to register for the Battle of the Bands. When should you get there? ____________________

b When can your family watch you play in the Battle of the Bands? ____________________

c You want to see the Harley Motor Bikes. When are they on? ____________________

d If you miss the bike parade, where can you see them afterwards? ____________________

e A friend of your family was in the Giant Cook-Up. When can you find out if she won? __________

f You have been helping a young friend build a billy cart for the Derby. When and where can you see him race? ____________________

g You are in the schools drama performance. Where do you perform? ____________________

h Your friend will be in the Grand Parade. When is it on? ____________________

i You have been involved in the new mural at the Youth Centre. When is it being unveiled? ________

j You want to spend some time at the Youth Centre doing activities. What times is it open? ________

Program of Events — Brooklands Gala Weekend

Time	Saturday	Sunday
9.30 am	Opening by City Mayor (Centre Stage) Brooklands City Band	
10 am	Registration for Battle of the Bands Competition — until 12 noon Jazz ballet performance (Town Square)	Assemble for Skateboard Competition (Skate Park) Children's Magic Show (Town Square)
10.30 am	Art exhibition opens (Scout Hall) All Grand Parade participants assemble in Brooklands Park	Local High Schools Drama Performances (Centre Stage)
11 am – 1 pm	Giant Cook-up — 10 local cooks battle it out for Brooklands Cook of the Year (Main Hall)	Skateboard Competition
11.30 am – 12.30 pm	Grand Parade — Starts in Brooklands Park	Harley Motor Bike and Vintage Car Parade. Starts Brookland Park

12.30 – 2 pm	Battle of the Bands — Under 18 division (Centre Stage)	Vintage Cars and Motor Bikes on display (Greens Road) — rides available Farm yard animals (Bligh Park)
2 pm	Demonstration of Martial Arts (Town Square) Winner of Giant Cook-up announced (Centre Stage)	Billy Cart Derby (Car Park behind Railway Station)
2.30 – 3 pm	Dog Show (Brooklands Park)	Unveiling of Mural 'Our Place' (Brooklands Youth Centre)
3 pm – 4 pm	Battle of the Bands — Over 18 division (Centre Stage) Youth Centre open for sport and recreation activities (until 8 pm)	Youth Centre open for sport recreation activities (until 6 pm)
3.30 pm	Snake Man Show (Bligh Park)	Official close of Gala Weekend
4 pm	Winners of Battle of the Bands announced — Centre Stage	
5 pm – 9 pm	Food Festival (Brooklands Park)	
6 pm – 9 pm	Open Air Concert (Brooklands Park)	

2 Read each question about the text *Some endangered species* on the following page and then find the answer to the question as quickly as you can. *Do not* read the whole text — scan for the answers to the questions *only*.

a How many species are *critically endangered*? ____________________

b How many sub-species of Asian elephant are endangered? ____________________

c What is the estimated population of the northern hairy-nosed wombat? ____________________

d How much has the population of the African elephant declined over the last three generations?

____

e Where are giant armadillos found? ____________________

f How many right whales are thought to remain in the world's oceans? ____________________

g Where is the Asiatic cheetah found? ____________________

h What reason is given for the decline in giant panda population? ____________________

i How many sub-species of tigers are there? ____________________

Some Endangered Species

paragraph

There are more than 1,000 animal species endangered world-wide. An endangered species is one that is in immediate danger of becoming extinct if nothing is done to protect it. ('Immediate' is usually taken to mean between 10 and 20 years.) Below are some of the world's main endangered mammals. **1**

African elephant. Classified as endangered due to a reduction of at least 50% of the African elephant population over the last three generations. Hunting is now banned in many countries, but poaching for ivory continues. **2**

Asian elephant. Classified as endangered due to a reduction of at least 50% of population over the last three generations. Four sub-species affected: Indian, Ceylonese, Sumatran and Malaysian elephants. **3**

Right whale. Classified as endangered due to the fact that the population is estimated to be less than 250 mature right whales. Also, the estimated continuing decline is thought to be at least 20% within two generations. The right whale was once the most hunted of all whales but is now protected by law. **4**

Blue whale. Endangered classification due to reduction of at least 50% of population over last three generations. Largest mammal ever to have lived on Earth. **5**

Hybrid spider monkey. Classified as endangered due to the fact that it only exists in severely fragmented sub-populations, and continuing decline in population. Known for its ability to use its tail as an extra limb. **6**

Gorilla. Classified as endangered due to projected population figures getting no higher than 50% of present population. **7**

Red wolf. Critically endangered due to estimation that there are no more than 50 mature red wolves. **8**

Asiatic cheetah. Critically endangered based on estimation of less than 50 mature animals and a continuing decline in these numbers. Asiatic cheetahs are found in Iran. **9**

Tiger. Classified as endangered based on projected population figures of no more than 50% of current population, and significant decline in habitat. Eight sub-species, but only five are endangered. **10**

Giant panda. Classified as endangered due to fact that it exists in scattered populations of only 250 mature adults in total. Continuing erosion of habitat as forests in China have been cut down for settlement and agriculture. **11**

Northern hairy-nosed wombat. Critically endangered. Estimated population of less than 50 mature individuals in Australia (only place found). **12**

Giant armadillo. Estimated population decline of at least 50% over past ten years. Only found in South America. **13**

Predicting

WHAT?

Whenever you read, you are constantly **predicting** in your head the next word, the next sentence, the next paragraph, the next chapter.

Mostly you are unaware that you are doing this, but the more you are *actively* thinking about what comes next, the more you will get from the text.

You predict both *before* you start to read a text, and *while* you are reading.

HOW?

You predict by

- using what you know about the world. If you read the sentence *The baby couldn't eat the apple because he didn't have any* _______ , you can guess that the next word will be *teeth* because of what you know about babies.
- using what you know about language. In the sentence above, you can guess that the next word will probably be a noun (a name for a person or thing). You know it won't be *about* or *often* or *the* because these words do not make sense after the word *any*.
- using visuals — photographs, drawings, charts. For example, you can predict the main ideas of a newspaper article by looking at the photographs.
- using headings or sub-headings. Newspaper headlines, for example, capture in a few words the main point of the story.
- using everything you have read so far in the text. For example, you can sometimes predict what is going to happen in a story based on what you have read.

Of course you can't always predict *exactly* what is coming, so it does not matter if your predictions are not right. The important thing is to be thinking constantly about what might be coming next. Don't only think about the word or sentence your eyes are focusing on.

In other words, be an *active* reader, not a passive one.

WHY?

You predict when you read simply because you are human. Every minute of the day you are predicting and making guesses about what people will say or do, what will happen next and so on.

If you didn't constantly make predictions and guesses about the world, you probably wouldn't survive it for long. If you are not predicting as you read, and only concentrating on the word or sentence you are reading at the time, you will probably not understand the text completely.

There are many predicting tasks in Part Two. Usually they are in the 'Preparing to Read' sections. Make sure you do these. They will get you into the habit of thinking about what you are about to read.

PRACTICE

answers page 129

The predicting activities below will make you aware of how we predict as we read, and give you practice in developing the skill.

1 You are travelling on a bus and quickly glance at the newspaper the man next to you is reading. You only see the following words before he turns the page:

skateboards	warns	injuries
50,000 hospital visit	90% under 15	particularly at risk
less strength	children under 10	learn about risky behaviour

Guess from these few words, if the article is about: (tick one)

a ___ a plan to ban skateboarding in local streets and parks

b ___ the risks of skateboarding for children

c ___ a new plan to make skateboarding an organised sport

d ___ a serious skateboarding accident that recently occurred

2 Here are the headings from a chapter in a book about animal behaviour.

Animal perception	What is colour	Evolution's paintbox	Borrowing a coat
White for winter	Matching the surroundings	Invisible fish	Deceiving the eye

What do you think the chapter might be about? ______________________________

3 Match each of these short story titles (**a–e**) to the first sentences below (**i–v**) that you predict might belong to them.

a Food Chain

b The Kidnapper

c Dad, Mum, the Circus and Me

d Streetkid

e The Storm

i If Julia hurried she would just get home in time. She couldn't remember an afternoon like this.

ii The trapdoor closed with a thud. Rosie was alone.

iii The rat tensed his muscles. It was dangerous down here in the waterpipes.

iv When Dad died we were left high and dry.

v Light poured from the sole streetlight. Joel hugged the shadows as he made his way to the corner store.

4 The newspaper article below has had all the punctuation taken out. Read the article and put full-stops, commas and inverted commas (' …') back in so that it makes sense. To do this activity you will have to read *actively*, predicting where sentences are likely to stop and start.

> A young surfer has escaped unscathed after a three-metre shark repeatedly attacked his surfboard taking a large chunk out of it Michael Brown 17 was surfing with two friends off Scotchy Head when the shark probably a bronze whaler attacked about 6.30 am Sunday it charged his board throwing him into the air the youth regained the board but as he and his friends struggled to catch a wave back to shore the shark attacked again biting a large chunk out of it the three managed to reach the beach unhurt later that day the boys were relaxing at home with family and friends enjoying being the centre of attention for the day however they warned all surfers to take special care when surfing just because shark attacks are rare doesn't mean they don't ever happen said Michael the three friends also stressed the need to surf with your mates it is just stupid to go out alone said Michael

5 **WARNING: This is a difficult activity, but give it a try.**

Read the first sentence on the left, and then read the three sentences on the right (**a**, **b**, **c**). Choose the one that you think would be most likely to follow that first sentence. Then move to the next sentence on the left and check your prediction. Repeat the process for each sentence in the left-hand column.

IMPORTANT: BEFORE YOU START, get a strip of paper and use it to cover up the sentences below the ones you are working on.

People can try to interpret their dreams.	**a** You should always try to remember them. **b** But to do that one has to remember them, and most dreams vanish before the end of the morning first's yawn. **c** Dreams are always difficult to remember.
But to do that one has to remember them, and most dreams vanish before the end of the morning's first yawn.	**a** Some dream experts suggest putting a pen and paper by your bed. **b** Think about the meaning of your dream. **c** Write them down before you get out of bed.
Some dream experts suggest putting a pen and paper by your bed.	**a** Think about what you have written down. **b** Dream experts don't realise how hard this. **c** As soon as you wake, you should write down any recollections before you do anything.
As soon as you wake, you should write down any recollections before you do anything.	

6 Now do the same for these sentences from the same text.

To interpret what your dream meant, think about the area of your life the dream was about.	**a** In general, we dream about things that are relevant to our own experiences. **b** Some people think that dreams are predictions about the future. **c** Some interesting research is coming out of America at present.
In general, we dream about things that are relevant to our own experiences.	**a** There are many kinds of dreams — falling, being chased, flying. **b** Experts warn that we should not be frightened of our dreams. **c** Another useful idea is to tell yourself before you go to sleep 'I will remember a dream tonight'.
Experts warn that we should not be frightened of our dreams.	**a** They are not instructions, just insights. What we do with the information is up to us. **b** Sleep patterns affect the way we remember our dreams. **c** Most of us dream about five times a night.
They are not instructions, just insights. What we do with the information is up to us.	

Working out word meanings

WHAT?

You often have to **work out the meanings of words** that you do not know. Most of the time you need to do this *without* a dictionary or another person to help you.

Sometimes you will only need to work out a rough meaning. At other times it will be important to work out an exact meaning.

HOW?

To work out meanings of new words, you

- use context clues. You look at the words that come before and after the word, and use the clues to work out the new word. If you read *The tiger is found in many different habitats: tropical forests, woodlands, grass jungles and even alpine regions*, you can probably work out that *habitats* means the kinds of places that animals live in.
- use knowledge of similar words. Knowing the word *inhabit* would also help you work out *habitat* in the sentence above.
- use knowledge of word parts. If you know that *mono* means *single* or *one*, and that *chrome* has something to do with colour, you can work out that *monochrome* means *using one colour*.

The most important of these strategies is **using context clues**. Even if you use other strategies, you will generally be using context clues at the same time.

WHY?

You can never know the meaning of every word in the English language, so you will quite often have to make guesses to work out meanings. Also,

- it's not a good idea to *always* rely on a dictionary or another person. This interrupts your reading and doesn't help you develop your own guessing skills.
- you don't always need the exact meaning of a word to be able to keep on reading.

It *is* a good idea, however, to check your guesses in a dictionary or with another person when you have finished reading. This will help to develop your vocabulary.

There are activities which ask you to work out word meanings in almost every text in Part Two. This is because it is such an important reading skill.

PRACTICE

answers page 129

These activities will make you aware of how much we can find out about a word's meaning from the context, and give you practice in using this skill.

1 Read the following paragraph and try to guess the meaning of the word *blip*.

> The *blip* is perhaps the most important invention of all time. The *blip* first appeared in Mesopotamia in modern Iraq, over 5000 years ago. These early *blips* were solid and cut from wooden planks which were then fastened together by wooden or metal cross-pieces. In some places where wood was scarce, stone was used for *blips* instead. They were very heavy, but at least they lasted a long time. *Blips* with spokes appeared much later, from around 2000 BC. This kind of *blip* was far more successful because it was so much lighter. From this point on, metal was used to stop wear and tear on the *blip* rims and to strengthen the *blip* structure. Bearings, which allowed the *blips* to turn more easily, appeared around 100 BC.

Blip is being used instead of the word: ______________________________

2 The following text has some words missing. Can you fill in the blanks with words from the box? To do this you will have to look closely at the words before and after the missing words.

appear	assaulted	sight
foot	office	stole
allegedly	ringing	hiding
charged	sound	ground
doing	hiding	officer

Mobile gives game away

A ringing mobile phone gave away the __________ place of a man who had allegedly __________ a female police officer yesterday. Police said the 23-year-old man ______________ a cash box from the front ______________ of a caravan park at Adelie Beach on the North Coast. He then ________ pushed the officer to the __________ after she asked him what he was __________ , and fled on ______________ into thick bushland behind the beach. A second ______________ gave chase but lost ______________ of the suspect.

Then the officer heard a mobile phone ______________ quite nearby. He followed the ________ and found the man ______________ behind a large rock. The man was arrested and _________ with stealing, assault, and resisting arrest and will ______________ in Portland Court on March 12.

3 Read these extracts from a text about communication, taking special note of the words in *italics*. Then decide which of the given words (**i–iii**) is closest to the meaning of the italicised word as it is used in the extract.

a The *advent* of the telephone improved interpersonal communications in many ways. It made it possible, for example, for a boy and a girl to get together without getting on a horse and riding miles to have a personal conversation.

i arrival **ii** purchase **iii** history

b The *impact* of the Internet has been far-reaching. It is changing the way we communicate, work, trade, entertain and learn. It might even be changing the way we think.

i importance **ii** influence **iii** increasing use

c Email is convenient and *instantaneous* but it may well be contributing to a world where we rarely need to actually see each other.

i quick **ii** impersonal **iii** immediate

d Modern communication methods have led to a situation where true human interactivity has been almost totally *eliminated.*

i made to disappear **ii** stopped **iii** destroyed

e Emails can sometimes *be ambiguous*. People frequently misinterpret what they read because they cannot see or hear the other person.

i convey more than one meaning **ii** be insulting **iii** be too brief

4 Read these sentences about animal communication. In each case work out the meaning of the word in italics and write it down.

a The chimpanzee uses a rich combination of facial expressions, noises and *postures* to communicate.

____

b Researchers have mainly worked with *captive* chimps because of the difficulty of working in the wild.

____

c Chimps must be *accustomed to* contact with people from birth in order to be taught any human language successfully.

____

d While animals use a variety of communication methods, for many, the most *flexible* method of communication is sound.

____

e The South American tree frog *amplifies* its call by expanding its throat sac.

____

f Recent research shows chimps and spider monkeys *aping* the behaviour of their human cousins.

____

g Scientist *speculate* that the song of the humpback whale may be a subtle kind of language.

____

h Researchers have to distinguish between behaviour that is common to all the species and behaviour that is *idiosyncratic.*

____

i Orangutans in Western Borneo express annoyance by pressing a leaf against their *pursed* lips to make a kissing sound.

____

Understanding writer's purpose and text organisation

5

WHAT?

When you read information texts it is important to understand the writer's purpose. Are they, for example

- explaining how something happens or works?
- describing something?
- arguing for or against an idea?
- discussing ideas?
- comparing and contrasting two things?
- recounting what happened and when?
- classifying or categorising things (e.g. animal species)?

To understand the purpose, you need to take notice of how the writer has organised their ideas. If the purpose is to tell what happened, the writer will probably organise the ideas in chronological (time) order. If the purpose is to explain a scientific phenomenon (e.g. global warming), the writer will probably talk about the causes and effects of this phenomenon.

In fiction texts the overall purposes and ways of organising text are less predictable.

HOW?

To understand the writer's purpose and how a text is organised, it helps to

- read the text introduction carefully. This usually gives you a big clue to the overall purpose of the text.
- take special notice of linking words. If you see words like *From then on ...*, *In 1989 ...*, *During the year ...* , you will see that the writer's purpose is to tell what happened and when.
- take special notice of the topic sentences (usually the first sentences in paragraphs). The topic sentence should give clues about the purpose of the paragraph as well as the content. For example, if a paragraph begins: *There are many differences between ...* , you can be pretty sure the purpose of the paragraph is to compare and contrast two things.

WHY?

Paying attention to the writer's purpose and how the text is organised helps you to see it as *one whole thing* not as a series of unrelated bits and pieces. It is essential for understanding the main ideas in a text.

There are a number of activities in Part Two which get you to focus on how the ideas are organised.

PRACTICE

answers page 130

Do these activities to make you more aware of text purpose and organisation.

1 **a** Read the text below. What is the writer's purpose? (Choose one.)

i to argue for or against an idea

ii to tell what happened

iii to compare and contrast facts or ideas

Spiders and insects may look a little alike and share some characteristics. Both are invertebrates, and belong to a division of the animal kingdom called the arthropods. As part of this group, they both have exoskeletons (hard external skeletons), segmented bodies and jointed limbs. On top of this, of course, both have rather bad reputations for biting and stinging human beings!

However, there are clear differences between the two. The body of a spider is divided into two sections, whereas an insect's body is divided into three. The spider has four pairs of walking legs compared to the insect's three pairs. Spiders usually have only simple eyes (six to eight) while insects have both compound and simple eyes. Spiders lack the antennae and wings that most insects have. Spiders have silk glands in their abdomens and spinnerets to weave their webs. Insects have neither of these features. Spiders do not have true jaws as insects do, and so they feed by a sucking action after poisoning and pouring digestive juices on their prey.

b Now fill in the summary chart below. (You do not need to write full sentences.)

	Spiders	Insects
Similarities		
Differences		

2 **a** Read this short text. What is the writer's purpose? (Choose one.)

i to describe something

ii to compare and contrast facts or ideas

iii to explain how something works

The body of an insect is divided into three parts: head, thorax and abdomen. The head has one pair of antennae, one pair of compound eyes, up to three simple eyes, and various mouth parts to enable piercing, sucking or chewing, depending on the insect's feeding habits. The thorax is divided into three segments, each with a pair of jointed legs. Many insects develop wings on the second and third segments in adulthood. The abdomen may be made up of up to eleven parts, with the tip perhaps adapted for mating or stinging.

b Now draw a simple diagram to show the important information in the insect text in **2a** above. (Don't worry about the eyes.)

3 **a** Read the short text below. What is the writer's purpose? (Choose one.) Use the words in *italics* to help you.

i to argue for or against an idea

ii to explain how or why something happens

iii to tell what happened

A major *reason* that tigers are classified as endangered is habitat loss. Across Asia, vast forests have been felled for timber, for agricultural land and for human settlement. *This has led to* a situation where only small islands of forest surrounded by villages and towns are left. *As* the forest space is reduced, the number of animals of all kinds left in the forest is also reduced, and tigers cannot find the prey they need for survival. *As a result*, tigers begin to eat the livestock of villagers who live near them, or even the villagers themselves. *In turn*, the villagers sometimes kill the tigers in order to protect themselves. *Another consequence* of the forest clearing process is that tigers become separated from each other by the new villages and farms that take the forest's place. *This leads to* inbreeding as tigers mate repeatedly with the same small group. Over time, this weakens the gene pool and tigers are born with birth defects.

b Use a simple flowchart (boxes and arrows) to take notes of the main points of the text in **3a**.

4 The text below tells what happened and when it happened. Use the words in *italics* and other clues to put the sentences in the right order. (Write the letters **a–e** as your answer.) Begin with sentence **d**.

a Julio's tag *was quickly followed* by 'Taki 183' which turned out to be the tag of a young Manhattan man called Demetrius.

b *Around that time,* the words 'Julio 204' *first* began appearing all around New York city.

c *Within a year* of the article on Taki 183 appearing, hundreds of new writers emerged and took New York City by storm.

d Art in the form of graffiti originated *in the late 1960s,* though graffiti in the form of words or drawings scratched on walls to express an idea had been around for a long time before then.

e *In 1971,* the New York Times found and interviewed Taki 183 to try and explain the new phenomenon.

____

Understanding main ideas 6

WHAT?

Understanding the main ideas means seeing through all the detailed ideas on the page to understand what the writer is really getting at. It's seeing how the 'bits and pieces' fit together.

It is like looking at a photograph made up of thousands of black, grey and white dots, and being able to work out what the subject of the photograph is.

It also involves being able to distinguish the main ideas from the details which support them.

HOW?

To understand the main ideas in non-fiction you need to:

- see each sentence as part of a larger whole. Don't focus only on the meaning of the sentence you are reading.
- pay attention to the text introduction. It will often tell you the main idea of the whole text.
- pay attention to topic sentences (usually, the first sentences of the paragraphs). These should state the main ideas of the paragraphs.
- think about how general or how specific statements are. *Soccer requires great skill* is a very general statement. *The best soccer players are very fast* is a more specific one. *Harry Kewell is one of the fastest soccer players the world has seen* is even more specific.
- take notice of linking words — words like *however, for example, as a result, in contrast* and so on. Also take notice of words that refer back to something in the previous sentence, e.g. *this, the, those.*
- ask yourself if you really understand what the writer is getting at. If you don't, read the text again.

In fiction — novels, short stories and poems for example — you have to work harder to get the writer's point. It won't be clearly stated in an introduction or perhaps anywhere in the text at all. Also, novels and short stories very often use paragraphs with no clear topic sentences. Poetry makes no use of topic sentences at all — the writer uses other techniques to get the main ideas across.

WHY?

The only time that understanding the main ideas is *not* so important is when you scan for a specific bit of information. Otherwise, it is an important part of *all* the reading that you do.

There are a number of activities in Part Two which give you practice in understanding main ideas.

PRACTICE

answers page 131

The activities below will make you more aware of what you need to pay attention to in understanding the main ideas of a text.

1 Finding the most general statement in a paragraph is often the key to understanding the main idea. Number these simple statements from the most general (1) to the most specific (4).

Example

i __2__ We eat ice-cream at least three times a week.
ii __4__ My father hides the ice-cream at the back of the freezer so that we won't find it.
iii __3__ My father is an absolute ice-cream addict.
iv __1__ Everyone in my family loves ice-cream.

a **i** ____ Your skin is waterproof.
ii ____ Your skin is an all-purpose covering.
iii ____ Your insides need to be kept moist so that they don't stop working.
iv ____ Skin keeps water out, and more importantly, it keeps water in.

b **i** ____ Our faces are windows into our thoughts and feelings.
ii ____ Something in our faces signals whether, for example, we are lying or not.
iii ____ The psychologist travelled the world looking at faces in all kinds of culture.
iv ____ One US psychologist set out to discover the rules that govern how we interpret facial expressions.

2 Sequencing tasks help to make you aware of how sentences link together to express a main idea. Sequence the sentences below so that they form one whole paragraph. Use the words in *italics* to help you. The first two have been done for you.

a __2__ *This* is not surprising given that when we are frightened or upset our heart starts thumping.

b ______ *Today we know* that the heart is just a muscular pump for the blood.

c ______ *But* the belief turned out to be wrong.

d __1__ *In the past,* people used to think that the heart controlled the whole body including feelings and emotions.

e ______ *What is more,* we know that the whole body is controlled by this amazing organ.

f ______ *This* old belief gave rise to phrases like 'I know it in my heart'.

g ______ *We know* that the heart is in fact controlled by the brain.

3 Sequence these sentences below in the same way. Again take notice of the words in italics. The first one has been done for you.

a ______ *Two in three, for example,* would talk to their mothers about failing exams whereas one in three would talk to their fathers.

b __1__ *A recent study* of Australian youth has some good news for mothers around the country.

c ______ *And* more than half would tell mum if they were worried about something while only one-quarter would tell dad.

d _______ *Mothers* were nominated *more than twice* as often as fathers *overall* as the person they would talk to.

e _______ *The survey* of 400 young people between 8 and 15 showed that young people think that *mothers* are better than fathers to talk to about most topics.

4 Read this text on research into humour and then complete the summary of the main ideas. You can use words from the text but in some cases you will have to use your own words. (NOTE: there are more questions about this text in the next Key Skill, Understanding detail, p. 27.)

Growing Up Laughing

paragraph

Laughter is a funny business. It's part of human behaviour all over the world, regardless of culture. It makes us less stressed, lowers our blood pressure and reduces anxiety. Yet it remains one of the least understood aspects of human behaviour. **1**

Not all laughter is a response to humour. We laugh when we are nervous or embarrassed, or when we are relieved about something. We very often laugh at things that we don't really think are funny. In a social group, for example, we might laugh after someone says something fairly ordinary and without any humour. We laugh because it helps to 'oil the social wheels' — keep the conversation going and make everyone feel part of a group. **2**

There have been a number of research studies into laughter in recent years. One British investigation focused on how we develop our sense of humour. This study expected to prove that our sense of humour had more to do with our genes than our upbringing. Many personality traits seem to be determined by our genes,so the researchers suspected that the same might apply to sense of humour. **3**

The team tested the humour of 71 pairs of identical twins and 56 pairs of fraternal twins (non-identical) who had been raised together. They asked each pair to go into separate rooms and rate five cartoons from Gary Larson's *The Far Side* on a scale from zero (not at all funny) to 10 (one of the funniest ever seen). **4**

The results showed that siblings tend to have similar views on what is funny. The important thing though was that identical twins who have exactly the same genes, were no more likely to agree on this than fraternal twins who share only about half their genes (like ordinary siblings). What this suggests is that it is a shared environment, not shared genes, that makes brothers and sisters laugh at the same things. **5**

The finding surprised the research team. However, they suggested it might explain why different nationalities find quite different things funny. What is hilariously funny in one country, can go down like a lead balloon in another. This could be because of the shared environment that people experience when growing up in a particular country. **6**

Laughter is part of human ___________ all over the world, yet it is not very well _________ . We laugh for a variety of____________ , not only because we find something _________ . One recent study set out to discover how we develop our sense of humour, and expected to find that it was to do with our ___________ not our upbringing. The study tested the responses of fraternal and __________ twins to a set of cartoons. They found that twins in _______ groups tended to have similar views to their siblings about what was funny. The interesting thing was that ______ twins were no more likely to agree than the ___________ twins. This suggests that shared genes played no part but shared __________ did. The surprising results might explain the cultural ___________ in senses of humour.

5 **a** The text on kissing which appeared on page 5 is reprinted below. All the ideas below are mentioned in the text. Next to each, write whether the idea is a main idea (**M**) or a supporting or unimportant detail (**S**).

- **i** _____ Cavemen used to lick their neighbours' cheeks for the salt.
- **ii** _____ Kissing has been around since very early times.
- **iii** _____ Ancient Greek and Roman parents kissed their children.
- **iv** _____ Images of Christ were kissed to show devotion.
- **v** _____ There are many kinds of kisses.
- **vi** _____ The Mafia kiss of death is one grim kind of kiss.
- **vii** _____ Kissing rules and attitudes are different across cultures.
- **viii** _____ Kissing between men is common in Russia.
- **ix** _____ Kissing is becoming more common in Asia in recent times.
- **x** _____ Kissing appears to be on the increase as a social gesture.

b Now tick the statement above that you think is the main idea of the whole text. Look again at the text title to help you.

The Great Kissing Epidemic

paragraph

One theory is that it all began when cavemen began licking their neighbours' cheeks for the salt on them. But whatever its origins might have been, the fact remains that, in one form or another, kissing has been prevalent since primitive times, though it developed mostly in the West. **1**

Ancient Greek and Roman parents kissed their children, and lovers or married people kissed each other, as did friends of the same or different sex. In the Middle Ages knights kissed before doing battle, just as boxers touch gloves today before they begin the bout. Relics and images of Christ and the saints were often kissed to express reverence and devotion. **2**

The varieties of kisses are indeed numerous. There is the kiss of treachery (Judas' kiss is an example of this); the Mafia kiss of death has its own grim significance; the kiss of religious reverence is still a common sight in churches; and there is the kiss 'to-make-it-better', the kiss for luck, the kiss of greeting and the kiss of love. **3**

Kissing is very much a cultural practice and rules and attitudes vary across the **4**
globe. The French, who have had quite a lot of practice, have turned kissing into a fine social art, although these days, even they are not sure when or how to do it. The French double kiss is routine, but many French kiss one another three, or even more, times. It can sometimes go on for an embarrassingly long time. Italians are enthusiastic kissers at all times, and they have been for generations, if not for centuries. Arabic men greet one another with kisses, as do Arabic women. Russian men too are often seen greeting one another with kisses, and it is especially noticeable in the world of Russian politics, where the three-kiss greeting has become the norm. The British, though, remain shy about social kissing. The Japanese, along with many Asian peoples, regard kissing, at least in public, as a Western custom, unhygienic and sometimes even offensive. Kissing has, however, become more commonplace in some Asian countries in the past few decades.

But, despite the resistance of the British, and the opposition of some Eastern **5**
countries, kissing does seem to be on the increase as a social gesture. According to some sociologists, increased kissing is part of a general 'inflation' of intimate social signals. In other words, we kiss people we used to hug, we hug people we used to shake hands with, and we shake hands with those we used to nod to.

Understanding detail

7

WHAT?

Understanding the detail means understanding the 'bits and pieces' in a text. It means looking beyond the main idea and taking notice of all the smaller facts and ideas that support that idea.

HOW?

To understand the detail, you need to

- take time to fully understand every sentence. Don't skip a sentence because it looks too long and complicated.
- take notice of words that link ideas across sentences, e.g. in *contrast, although, moreover, nevertheless.*
- take notice of words such as *the, this, these, those, such, the other.* They also link ideas across sentences.
- try guessing the meanings of new words. If you can't, and the word looks really important, use your dictionary or ask someone what it means.
- read back over parts of the text that you did not understand the first time.

Of course, most of us *do* skip over at least *some* detail at least *some* of the time.

Still, it is easy to be caught out. How many times have you skipped some detail, then realised later that you *did* need it and had to go back and search for it before going on?

WHY?

Understanding detail is not always important but you do need to know when it *is* important and then make sure you pay attention to it when reading.

In fiction, understanding detail can be most important because the main idea might not be directly stated. You have to put all the details together and work out what this main idea is.

In this book, there are many tasks which require you to understand the detail. Always check your answers and then read back over the text if your answers are wrong.

PRACTICE

answers page 131

These activities will raise your awareness of the skills needed to understand detail.

1 Read the text below and answer the questions about the parts in *italics.*

> The ancient Egyptians believed that it was important to record and communicate information about religion and government. *Thus*, they invented written records that could be used to record *this information*. The most famous of all ancient Egyptian scripts is hieroglyphic. However, throughout 3,000 years of ancient Egyptian civilisation, at least *three other scripts* were used for different purposes. Using these scripts, scribes were able to preserve the beliefs, history and ideas of ancient Egypt in temple and tomb walls and on papyrus scrolls. Today *their work* provides us with a wonderful window into the past.

a What is another word you could use for *thus* in the text? ______________________

b What is *this information*? ______________________

c ' ... at least *three other scripts* were used for different purposes.' Three other scripts besides what?

____

d 'Today *their work* provides us with ...' Whose work? ______________________

2 Now do the same for this text.

> Records of writing provide valuable insights into ancient ways of life, but archeologists have to distinguish carefully between what are true records and *what are not*. While records of accounts and trading details may generally be accurate, records of historical events or the actions of rulers *may not be*. One indication of *this* is that records of battles that rulers have lost are very rarely found.

a ' ... have to distinguish carefully between what are true records and *what are not*.' Not what?

____

b ' ... records of historical events or the actions of rulers *may not be*.' May not be what?

____

c 'One indication of *this* ...' Indication of what?______________________

3 Read this text carefully and answer the questions. Use your dictionary to confirm meanings of words you are not sure of.

Egyptian hieroglyphics had long been a great mystery to the world's scholars, with virtually all understanding of this script being lost in the 4th century AD. Then in July, 1799, an irregularly shaped slab of black basalt was found near the mouth of the Nile River, in Egypt, by a soldier in a French fort established by Napoleon's army. The soldier and his companions observed that the stone bore inscriptions in three different scripts — one of which appeared to be Egyptian hieroglyphics. They rightly supposed that the three scripts were probably three versions of the same text. Because one of the scripts was in Greek and therefore could be read, they realised the potential importance of the stone for the decipherment of Egyptian hieroglyphics.

Upon news of the discovery, the Rosetta Stone (as it is now known) immediately became a subject of extreme interest and excitement amongst scholars around the globe. Once copies of the text were distributed, the Greek was translated and the Stone was found to be a text written by high priests in Egypt to honour the Egyptian Pharoah of the time (the 13-year-old Ptomely V Epiphanes). It recorded all the benefits that the Pharoah had conferred on the Egyptian people. The inscription between the Greek and the hieroglyphics was identified as a cursive form of hieroglyphic writing — an abbreviated and modified form.

However, no progress was made in the decipherment of either of the Egyptian versions till about 20 years later. While many linguistic experts worked on translating the hieroglyphics from the Greek, the final breakthrough was made by a Frenchman, Jean-Francois Champollion, in 1822, with substantial help from earlier discoveries by Thomas Young. Champollion was a brilliant linguist who began his work on the Rosetta Stone in 1808 when he was only 18. After 14 years of study, he finally broke the code completely and published his results.

a When was understanding of hieroglyphics lost? ______________________________

b When was the slab of basalt found? ______________________________

c Who found the slab of basalt? ______________________________

d Why was this person in the area? ______________________________

e How many scripts were found on the slab of basalt? ______________________________

f Which script could be read? ______________________________

g Why did the soldiers think the stone was important? ______________________________

h What is the stone now called? ______________________________

i What was the purpose of the writing on the Stone? ______________________________

j What was listed in the writing? ______________________________

k How many years after the discovery of the stone were the hieroglyphics deciphered? ____________

l Who deciphered the hieroglyphics? How long did it take him? ____________

m Whose work helped him? ____________

4 Look back at the questions in **3** above. Put a cross next to those you think are the three most important ideas in the text. (For example, **c** is not so important, but **g** is quite important.)

5 Look again at the text about laughter and answer these questions about the detail.

Growing Up Laughing

paragraph

Laughter is a funny business. It's part of human behaviour all over the world, regardless of culture. It makes us less stressed, lowers our blood pressure and reduces anxiety. Yet it remains one of the least understood aspects of human behaviour. **1**

Not all laughter is a response to humour. We laugh when we are nervous or embarrassed, or when we are relieved about something. We very often laugh at things that we don't really think are funny. In a social group, for example, we might laugh after someone says something fairly ordinary and without any humour. We laugh because it helps to 'oil the social wheels' — keep the conversation going and make everyone feel part of a group. **2**

There have been a number of research studies into laughter in recent years. One British investigation focused on how we develop our sense of humour. This study expected to prove that our sense of humour had more to do with our genes than our upbringing. Many personality traits seem to be determined by our genes,so the researchers suspected that the same might apply to sense of humour. **3**

The team tested the humour of 71 pairs of identical twins and 56 pairs of fraternal twins (non-identical) who had been raised together. They asked each pair to go into separate rooms and rate five cartoons from Gary Larson's *The Far Side* on a scale from zero (not at all funny) to 10 (one of the funniest ever seen). **4**

The results showed that siblings tend to have similar views on what is funny. The important thing though was that identical twins who have exactly the same genes, were no more likely to agree on this than fraternal twins who share only about half their genes (like ordinary siblings). What this suggests is that it is a shared environment, not shared genes, that makes brothers and sisters laugh at the same things. **5**

The finding surprised the research team. However, they suggested it might explain why different nationalities find quite different things funny. What is hilariously funny in one country, can go down like a lead balloon in another. This could be because of the shared environment that people experience when growing up in a particular country. **6**

a What is one example of how laughter affects us all in the same way?

____

b What are two reasons for laughing — besides finding something funny?

____

c What does it mean to *oil the social wheels*?

____

d The British study aimed to prove that …

____

e How do we develop many of our personality traits?

____

f How many non-identical twins were tested? ____________________

g Whose cartoons did the twins rate? ____________________

h The results were similar for both identical and fraternal twins. True or false? __________

i The results show that it was the shared environment not the shared genes that was more important.

True or false? __________

Understanding complex sentences

8

WHAT?

Often you will have no difficulty in understanding the sentences in a text. But even the most experienced reader will sometimes stumble over more **complex sentences**.

Sentences might be complex

- because they are very long
- because they consist of many parts
- because they contain many facts and ideas, or
- because of a combination of these factors.

HOW?

To understand complex sentences, you need to:

- take your time and read slowly. Read the difficult sentences twice, three times or as many times as you need to.
- read the difficult parts out loud. This often helps to make things clearer.
- work out the essential parts of the sentence. Work out what the subject of the sentence is (i.e. what or who the sentence is about), and the main verb (what that person or thing did).
- break up the sentences into smaller chunks of meaning.
- identify the main clause (the one that makes sense by itself) where there is more than one.
- don't skip sentences because they look long and complicated.

WHY?

Complex sentences occur in all kinds of writing. They are particularly common in information texts and in some kinds of newspaper articles.

While many texts written for school students are written quite simply, you'll often have to read texts written for an adult audience when you're researching an assignment topic. These texts will certainly include complex sentences.

In Part Two, there are many activities which require you to understand complex sentences in order to answer the questions.

PRACTICE

answers page 132

These activities will raise your awareness of the skills needed to understand complex sentences.

1 In these sentences underline the main **clause** — the clause that makes sense by itself. The clauses have been separated with '/'. Following are three examples.

<u>You can listen to radio</u> / while doing other things.

When an event is actually occurring, / <u>people usually turn on the radio first for information</u>.

<u>Radio is more accessible</u> / because it is easier to find one and turn it on.

a Radio can report on events / as they are happening.

b Because radio journalists need very little equipment, / radio can often be first with the news.

c Radio can abandon all its other programs / to concentrate on an important story / and to provide a community service.

d In bushfire disasters, radio informs people about the location of fires, / as well as running appeals / to collect clothing and food for people affected.

e Now that talkback radio is so popular, / almost every radio station in the country incorporates a talkback segment / to give listeners a chance to have their say.

2 In these sentences underline the noun which is the subject of the verb (in italics). Following are three examples.

Theme <u>music</u> usually *introduces* a news program.

The <u>newsreader</u> *reads* the introduction and *passes* the story to a reporter.

A <u>participant</u> in the event being reported *might tell* what happened or *offer* an opinion.

a News programs on most major TV channels *try* to cover news of national and international interest as well as local issues.

b Some news programs, especially those on commercial channels, *can appear* to be more interested in entertainment than information.

c Stories about lost kittens, cute children or unusual human behaviour *should not be allowed* to dominate news programs.

d A good example of the importance of conflict to news stories *was* a recent item about a student protest.

e The competition between television channels to film the best pictures *is* intense.

f Most news programs, even those that regularly broadcast violent drama series, *will not show* film with victims of accidents, murders or wars.

3 Break these sentences into small chunks of meaning (about five or six words). Note: there is more than one way to do this.

e.g. Expensive publicity campaigns are run / which aim to convince people / that the news on one channel / is better than others / because the newsreader knows / what is going on in the world, / and is more reliable and trustworthy.

a With newspapers it is possible to flick through the pages, scan the headlines and the introductory paragraphs, read an article on one page and then go back and read another report in a different part of the paper.

b The newsreader's job is to introduce the news item and make it possible for a journalist to continue it with film that has been selected.

c The limited time for in-depth treatment of stories in the TV news means that TV viewers do not get as much detail as newspaper readers.

d Natural-sounding speech helps to create an impression that the newsreader and journalists are having a conversation with each viewer rather than talking to millions of viewers in a million different lounge rooms all at once.

9 Understanding graphs and tables

WHAT?

Writers often use graphs and tables to present large amounts of information within a small space. While graphs and tables can be helpful, they can be difficult to follow.

Most graphs are organised on a horizontal and a vertical axis. Some graphs are organised differently eg pie graphs, but these are usually easier to read.

Tables are also organised on a horizontal and a vertical axis, and in general you will use the same skills and strategies to read them.

HOW?

To understand most graphs and tables it is a good idea to

- look over the whole graph or table to get a general idea of what it is about. Pay special attention to headings and labels.
- look along the horizontal axis and the vertical axis to find out what kind of information is included. For example, in a graph showing average heights during childhood, you might find ages on one axis and heights on the other.
- use your fingers as much as you need to, to help you follow lines, bars, columns or rows from the two axes to points on the graph or table.
- focus on one bit at a time instead of trying to understand the whole graph or table. Put your finger on one place in the graph or table. Then use two fingers to work back to the horizontal and vertical axis.
- think about what the results mean overall and how they relate to your own knowledge. Ask yourself if they seem reasonable.
- take your time. Most people find graphs and tables a little difficult to read. Most people need their fingers at least some of the time!

WHY?

If there is a graph or table in a text, you will generally need to pay some attention to it.

Of course you may not need to understand every detail. But, if you don't understand its overall structure and layout, you won't understand anything.

Graphs and tables are very commonly used in information texts on all kinds of subjects so it is important that you try to understand them. They give you important detail about the main ideas in the texts, and help you to see the similarities and differences between different items and groups.

There some activities in Part Two which ask you to extract information from graphs and tables.

PRACTICE

answers page 132

The activities below will give you practice in reading graphs and tables.

1 Look at the graph below and answer the questions. Remember to use your fingers if you need to.

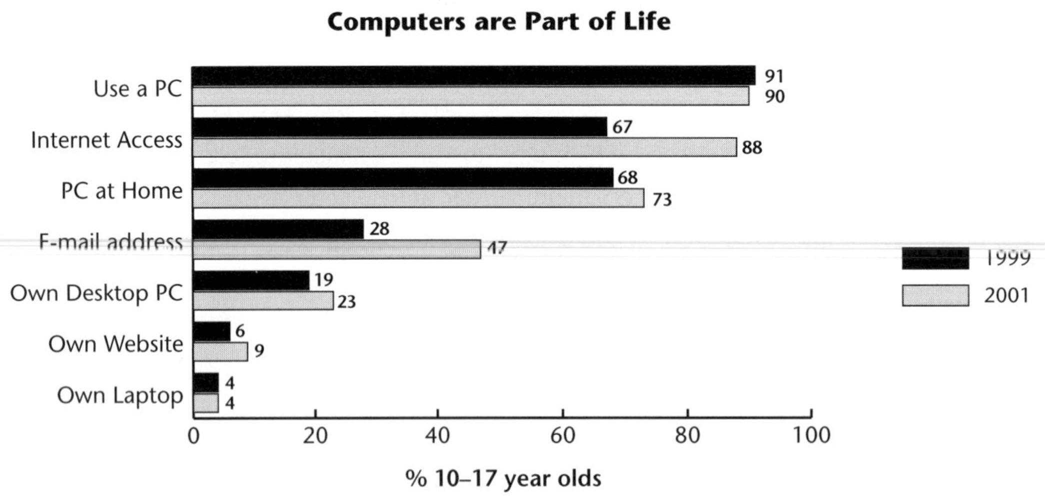

Reproduced with permission of Quantum Market Research

a In which years was the research done? ____________________

b Does the graph show what 10–17 year olds use computers for? ____________________

c How many 10–17 year olds had Internet access in 2001? ____________________

d Was this more or less than in 1999? ________ What was the difference between the two years?

____

e What does the figure of 47 mean? ____________________

f What increase is there over the two years in the percentage of 10–17 year olds who own their own desktop PC? ____________________

g Does the graph indicate an increase or decrease overall in computer use over the two years studied?

____

h Think about what you know about computer use amongst your age group at the moment. Would you say that the figures for this year would be different from these, or much the same?

____

In which ways? ____________________

____

2 Look at the graph below and answer the questions.

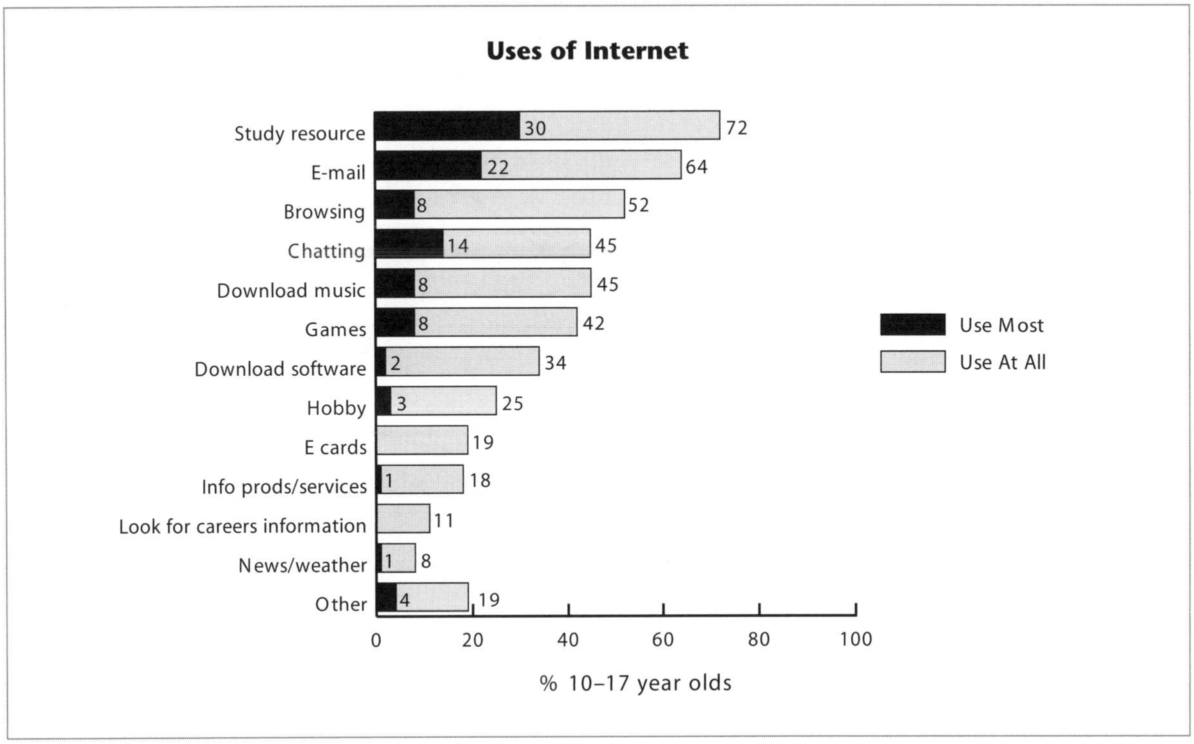

Reproduced with permission of Quantum Market Research

a How many uses for the Internet were found? ______________________

b The graph shows two kinds of information about Internet uses. What are they?

____

c What is the most common use of the Internet? ______________________

d What is the least common use of the Internet? ______________________

e What percentage of 10–17 year olds use the Internet mostly for study? ______________________

f What percentage use the Internet mostly for chatting? ______________________

g What percentage use the Internet for chatting at least sometimes? ______________________

h True or false? About a third of 10–17 year olds sometimes use the Internet for downloading software but very few do this regularly. ______________________

i Think about your own Internet use. Which would you say is your main use? ______________________
What else do you sometimes use the Internet for? (Underline the Internet uses listed on the left of the graph.)

3 Look at the graph below and answer the questions. (Note: There are usually 1,000 young people in Quantum Market Research studies.)

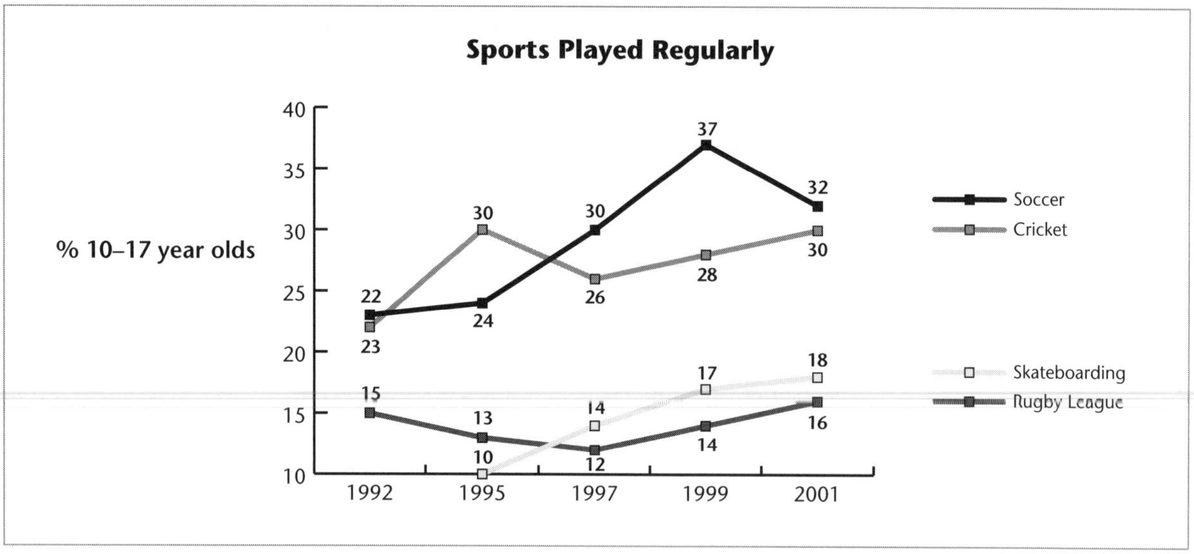

Reproduced with permission of Quantum Market Research

a The graph shows the percentage of 10–17 year olds interviewed that regularly play the four sports listed. True, false, or not clear? ____________________

b The graph shows the top four sports played regularly. True, false, or not clear? __________

c The most popular of the four sports in 1999 was soccer. True or false? __________

d Which two sports have shown the most growth since 1995? __________

e Which sport showed the most growth between 1992 and 1999? __________

f What percentage of 10–17 year olds played cricket in 1999? __________

g Overall, does the graph show an increase or decrease in participation in the four sports?

____

h The graph does not tell you if both boys and girls were interviewed. If both sexes were interviewed, what does this tell you about girls' participation in sport?

____

i Based on what you know about sports played by young people, do you think that both girls and boys were interviewed? Why/why not?

____

____

4 Look at the chart below and answer the questions.

Children aged 5–14 years
who participated in organised sport outside of school hours
during the 12 months before April 2000

Number				**Participation rate**		
	Males	Females	Persons	Males	Females	Persons
Swimming	177,000	203,100	380,100	13.1%	15.8%	14.4%
Soccer (outdoor)	265,000	37,300	302,300	19.6%	2.9%	11.4%
Netball	6,400	234,900	241,400	0.5%	18.2%	9.1%
Tennis	124,800	99,100	223,800	9.2%	7.7%	8.5%
Basketball	119,600	80,700	200,300	8.8%	6.3%	7.6%
Australian Rules football	170,300	4,100	174,400	12.6%	0.3%	6.6%
Cricket (outdoor)	133,600	7,300	140,900	9.9%	0.6%	5.3%
Martial arts	72,700	31,900	104,600	5.4%	2.5%	4.0%
Athletics	52,200	51,900	104,100	3.9%	4.0%	3.9%
Rugby League	92,500	2,500	95,100	6.8%	0.2%	3.6%

Source: Australian Bureau of Statistics, 'Participation in the most popular sports', from *Year Book Australia 2003, Culture and Recreation: Children's Participation in Cultural and Leisure Activities.* Australia, April 2000, publication 4901.0. Data used with permission from the Australian Bureau of Statistics (www.abs.gov.au).

a What sport was most played by boys in the 12 months before April 2000? ____________________

b What percentage of boys played this sport? ____________________

c What sport was most played by girls in the 12 months before April 2000? ____________________

d What percentage of girls played this sport? ____________________

e Did any girls play Rugby League? ____________________

f Did any boys play netball? ____________________

g What sport had about the same number of boys and girls participating? ____________________

h What does the figure 174,400 represent? ____________________

i Look back at the results of the Quantum Market Research in **3** above. In what ways do the results differ? ____________________

j Can you think of any reasons why the results might be different? ____________________

____

Inferring

10

WHAT?

Sometimes writers give you information or express ideas directly (or **explicitly**). At other times they convey their meaning indirectly (or **implicitly**). When this is the case you need to **infer** or **read between the lines**.

In fiction for example, a writer might describe the look on the face of a character and leave you to infer what this means about the character's thoughts and feelings. Or, a writer might leave you to work out what kind of person the character is from the dialogue.

In information texts too, writers do not always express ideas directly.

HOW?

To infer meaning you need to

- think about why certain detail is included, especially if it doesn't seem directly relevant. Writers usually have a good reason for including detail.
- think beyond the text. Relate what you read to your own personal, social and cultural experiences to help you understand it.
- look at sentences as part of the whole paragraph, not as isolated bits and pieces.
- pay close attention to dialogue in fiction texts. The writer will expect you to draw conclusions about the action and the characters from dialogue.

WHY?

Inferring is an essential part of reading. No writer tells you every single thing you need to know. If they did, every text would be three or four times as long as it is. Writers have to assume you can work out some things without being told about them directly.

Inferring is also an important part of critical reading (see next skill).

There are many tasks in Part Two which ask you to infer information and ideas from the text. Look carefully at the answers to these questions if you have any trouble doing them.

PRACTICE

answers page 132

These activities will give you practice at inferring. They will also make you aware how much you *do* understand when reading, without being explicitly told.

1 Fiction writers expect us to work out a fair bit about what is going on, even at the very start of their stories. Read the first paragraph below from a short story and then see how much you can work out.

> Michael woke up with a start. Someone was banging at the front door. Heavy footsteps clomped over the bare boards of the hallway. A shouting of voices. Jacko's familiar growl, then the front door slammed shut. Michael shivered and pulled the thin blanket closer around his shoulders. Through the cracked glass of the curtainless window, the sky looked grey and dirty. A groan from the other mattress told him that Toby was awake.
>
> (from 'Streetscape' by Ian Steep, in *Through the Web and Other Stories*, Harcourt Brace Jovanovich, 1992, p. 47)

Based on what you have read, answer the following questions.

a Who is Michael living with? ______________________________

b How long do you think Michael has lived there? Give your reasons. ______________________________

____

c What can you say about Jacko's mood? Which words tell you this?

____

d Would you say this mood is unusual or usual? Give your reasons.

____

____

e What kind of place are they living in? Which words tell you this?

____

____

f Why do you think Michael might be living in this place?

____

2 Now read this first paragraph from a novel, and see what you can work out.

> It was the sea-eagle that called Emily down to the beach. It hovered above the waves, its broad wings dusty where the land had left its mark, its small eyes that could follow the horizon bright and keen.
>
> She hadn't meant to come down onto the beach. She'd meant to sit at the top of the ramp till the other kids had left the street, till she could walk home in peace without strangers staring at her. But somehow the bird seemed to urge her to come down.
>
> (from *The Secret Beach* by Jackie French, Angus & Robertson, HarperCollins Publishers, 1995, p. 1)

a Where is the beach? (Circle one.)

in a small town | in a city suburb | on a deserted bit of coast

What makes you think this?

___

b What time of day do you think it is?

early morning | afternoon | evening

What makes you think this?

___

c In general, how do you think Emily feels?

happy | unhappy | bored

What makes you think this?

___

d Do you think Emily:

is on holidays at the beach? | has recently moved to the area? | has lived near the beach all her life?

What makes you think this?

___

3 Read this first paragraph from another novel and answer the questions which follow it.

> A single drop of water exploded on Pamela Browning's open exercise book. Pam started, sending an HB pencil skittering across her desk, and stared as the water spread over her carefully created map of Europe.
>
> Two hours' work destroyed. Pam throttled the pencil and stopped herself from hurling the exercise book away. Annabel was smiling sugar at her. Pam smiled thinly. They were friends; Annabel could not have seen the mess. Pam lifted her eyes and glared at the high, stained ceiling and dared it to throw another bomb at her.
>
> (from *Hero*, by Allan Baillie, Puffin Books, 1990, p. 7)

a Where was Pam? What makes you think this? ______________________________

____

b What kind of student is Pam? What makes you think this? ______________________

____

c What is happening outside the room? What makes you think this? ________________

____

d Pam says that she and Annabel are friends. What do you think (give reasons)? __________

____

e Do you think that Pam is upset only because her work is destroyed, and if not, what else could she be upset by? ____

____

4 Now read this information text. What evidence is there for the statements that follow it? Quote words from the text in your answer.

> Worldwide, approximately 10% of all reefs have been degraded beyond recovery, and it is estimated that 20–30% of the world's coral reefs could be destroyed in the next twenty years. Australian scientists do not want the Great Barrier Reef to be one of these. Unfortunately, however, the coral reefs and other marine life of the Great Barrier Reef are already under serious threat from excess fertiliser and sewage run-off, and from human activity in the area.
>
> The Great Barrier Reef is vital to the survival of thousands of species of marine life but also to the Australian tourism industry. It is rapidly deteriorating due to sewage and fertiliser run-off from sugar farming. The nutrients in this run-off encourage the growth of algae, which grow rapidly in nutrient-high waters. When the waters around the reefs become rich in nutrients, the algae take over and then smother and kill the coral. The nutrients also stunt the growth of many of the marine animals and plants, and eventually affect the number and diversity of fish, corals and other sea animals — the very things the tourists come to see.

a No attempt is being made to save some of the world's coral reefs.

____

____

b Australian scientists are working to save the Great Barrier Reef.

____

____

c The writer would support any effort to save the Great Barrier Reef.

____

____

d There are sugar farms near the coast.

____

____

e Tourists won't go to the reef if there is no coral or animal life to see.

____

____

Reading critically

11

WHAT?

Reading critically means that you do not simply accept everything you read as true, reliable or reasonable.

Facts may be left out or expressed in a particular way to suit the writer's view. Opinions may be biased or illogical. Or opinions may be expressed in a way that makes them sound more like fact.

Also, words may be used which make the reader think about the topic in the same way as the writer.

HOW?

To read critically you need to

- think about
  - why the writer wrote the text (purpose)
  - who they were writing to (audience) and
  - how they feel about the topic (attitude).
- take notice of who the author is. Is the author an expert? an ordinary member of the community? a journalist? a member of an organisation which supports a particular view?
- think about how the author's identity might influence what they have written.
- be wary of any texts where the author's name is not given.
- distinguish between what is fact and what is opinion.
- pay close attention to words which show the writer's attitude to a subject, e.g. *unfortunately, fortunately.*
- think about why a certain word has been used. For example, if you read about *noisy protesters*, you are likely to think differently about them than if you read simply *protestors.*

A good strategy when researching is to get your information from a range of texts. In this way, you will get a variety of writer views and attitudes.

WHY?

Every text is written by a person with a particular view on the topic being written about, and with a particular purpose in writing about that topic. You need to think about this more in some texts (e.g. newspaper articles) than in others.

However, even texts that appear to present no view at all may be encouraging the reader to think a certain way about the topic.

Reading critically is relevant in fiction too. Even though writers appear to be simply telling a story, they have made choices about what stories to tell, and what characters, situations, and plotlines to use. You need to think about these choices. This is part of interpreting the meaning of the book.

There are a number of critical reading activities in Part Two. You might find these questions difficult and prefer to do them with someone's help.

PRACTICE

answers page 133

These activities will make you more aware of how writers convey their view on a subject and encourage the reader to have a similar view.

1 Graffiti is one of the many subjects that people tend to have strong feelings about. These feelings come out in the language they choose when writing about the subject.

Read these statements which are taken from Letters to the Editor on the subject of graffiti.

a Street artists consider trains and streets as a gallery for their artwork.

b All concerned citizens will surely support the anti-graffiti squad in their fight against graffiti crime.

c Urban artists have decorated the wall by the local railway station.

d We need to take action against these criminals head-on.

e The battle against graffiti terrorists is on.

f Graffiti vandals should be made to confront their victims.

g Graffiti websites showcase the colourful and creative work of aerosol artists.

h These hoons aren't the ones who have to clean up their mess.

i Young people who do graffiti may not have any other opportunity to express their artistic ideas.

j One concerned gentleman at the anti-graffiti meeting suggested residents adopt an area to keep watch for graffiti vandalism.

k The young artists thanked the Mayor for the opportunity to do a graffiti mural at the community centre.

Now read them again. This time:

- Underline any words used to describe the people who do graffiti.
- Circle any words used to describe the people who do not do graffiti.
- Draw a wriggly line under any words used to describe the activity of doing graffiti.
- Write '+' if the writer is positive about graffiti, and '–' if the writer is negative.

e.g. (The community) does not want these <u>useless criminals</u> putting their ~ugly scribble~ on our walls and fences. (–)

As you do the activity, think about how the writer's choice of words could influence readers to have a similar view on the topic of graffiiti.

2 Look at these sentences about life on other planets and say if they are fact (**F**) or opinion (**O**).

Factual statements are statements we can prove or disprove by observation or experience. A factual statement may turn out to be inaccurate, but it is still *factual* rather than *opinion* if it can be *checked.* Statements of opinion may sound factual, but if there is no way to prove or disprove them, they are only opinion. (Note: Any statement about the future can only be opinion.)

a A giant football-shaped object floating across the city's skies last night was not a UFO. ________

b Over the past few decades, a growing number of astronomers have suggested that life on other planets is likely. ________

c Belief in extra-terrestrial life has led to hundreds of books and TV shows on the subject. ________

d The search for life on other planets is likely to fail. ________

e A new book claims we are not alone in the universe. ________

f Undoubtedly, searching for life on other planets is fascinating. ________

g There is debate in the scientific world about whether aliens would use radio or laser signals to communicate across galaxies. ________

h It is truly insane to think that there could be life on other planets. ________

i 40% of Americans believe in the possibility of life on other planets. ________

3 In the activities which follow you will be taken through a text on the search for extraterrestrial intelligence (SETI). The questions will make you focus on many aspects of critical reading.

a Read the first paragraph of the SETI text below.

> SETI is an abbreviation for the Search for Extraterrestrial Intelligence. It is the search for electromagnetic signals from other civilisations in the universe. At present there are a number of SETI projects operating at various observatories around the world. Most of these projects are searching for radio transmissions, but an increasing number of projects are now searching for light signals.

i Is the paragraph fact or opinion? ________________________________

ii Do you think the text which will follow this paragraph will present *information* about SETI or present a *view* on SETI? ________________________________

b Now read the next paragraph from the text.

> One especially useful project in operation is SETI@home. In this project, millions of individuals around the world use their personal computers to process radio data collected by SETI scientists via one radio telescope in Puerto Rico. The project distributes a free screensaver to all participants and in return gets to use the computing power of millions of computers worldwide.

What word tells you that the writer probably supports efforts to find life on other planets?

____

c Read the next two paragraphs.

It is reasonable to ask why anyone would conduct a SETI project. Well, the detection of another civilisation would clearly be one of the most important discoveries in the whole history of humankind. It would change forever our view of our place in the universe. Suddenly, we would be only one member of a community of intelligent species. We would have to rethink the history and evolution of our species and of our planet and this could only be to our benefit. It could be that it would also change the way we relate to each other on Earth. It could even lead to a more peaceful time as we begin to see ourselves as one whole community not a collection of many different communities.

It could be an extraordinary opportunity for mankind if we find that another civilisation has solved many of the problems we are still dealing with. On the other hand, such a discovery could be devastating to our sense of worth. We might find we are more or less primitive by comparison, and start to see ourselves very much as second-class citizens.

i Are the paragraphs fact or opinion? ______________________________

ii How many sentences are about positive outcomes of finding another civilisation? __________

iii How many sentences are about negative outcomes? ______________________________

iv Do you think the writer should have written more about negative outcomes? __________
Can you think of some negative outcomes of finding another civilisation on other planets?

____

v Which words tell you that the writer supports SETI? (e.g. *most important)* ______________

d Read the next paragraph.

So far there has been no convincing evidence found that life as we know it exists anywhere but on Earth. Not one radio signal from another planet has been detected. However, there is evidence that life forms on other planets may be possible. We know that life on Earth originated about four million years ago, only just after conditions became bearable for primitive life forms. So it does not seem impossible that life forms could have developed somewhere else, even in our own solar system. Also there have been discoveries of planets orbiting distant stars, and it seems only a matter of time till one similar to Earth could be found.

i How many lines are given to the lack of evidence of life on other planets? ______________

ii Is this information fact or opinion? ______________________________

iii How many lines are given to the possibility of life on other planets? ______________

iv Is this information fact or opinion? ________________________________

v What does this tell you about the writer? ________________________________

e Read the next paragraph.

> Some people claim that the US government is hiding proof of the existence of another civilisation on Mars, but this is absurd. There is simply no way that such knowledge could be kept secret. There are scientists all around the world carrying out searches for life on other planets, and all of these are communicating their findings to each other all the time. No government could control information under these conditions. And, you have to ask why they would want to. What is there to gain from covering up extraterrestrial life?

i The paragraph is mainly about the possibility of a government cover-up of aliens. Is it mainly fact or opinion? ________________________________

ii What argument for carrying on SETI research is hidden in this paragraph? ________________

____

f Read the final paragraph.

> Given our enormous fascination with the subject of extraterrestrials, SETI is likely to go on forever — or at least until some evidence is found that we are not quite alone in the big wide world.

How might the reader feel if they are not fascinated by SETI?

____

____

NOTE: In **3a** you probably said that you thought the text would present **information** about SETI not a **view** about it. Well, the text *did* give information, but you can probably now see how the writer also included a lot of opinion with that information. You can probably also see that the writer has a positive attitude towards SETI research and that this affects both what and how they wrote. (I am not saying SETI is stupid or wrong. Personally, I find the subject very interesting and would love to spend the day looking for ETs on my computer!)

Reading Texts part 2

In this part of the book, you'll get practice in applying the skills you learnt about in Part One.

You'll find a range of text types including novel extracts, newspaper reports and feature articles, information texts, and cartoons.

The topics too are varied, and, I hope, interesting – you'll read about rap music, cloning, pocket money, extreme sports and many other topics.

Preparing to read has one or two questions to encourage you to think about the text topic before you begin, or to quickly preview the text using skimming and/or predicting skills. Make sure you do these activities. They'll make your reading easier.

The point of this section is to get you thinking and reading actively. If you change your mind about your answers after reading the whole text, don't go back and change your answers, unless asked to.

Understanding the text is the biggest section. You should do this after you read the whole text unless told otherwise. You will find some of these questions harder than others. However you should have a go at them all and push yourself to your limits.

Responding to the text is a short section which usually asks you to do some writing in response to the ideas and information in the text. It encourages you to think about what you have read and what it means to you.

Spotlight on language Some texts also include a **Spotlight on language**. These sections draw your attention to a language technique or feature used in the text.

You can do the texts in any order you wish. There is one exception to this: many of the novel extracts are presented in two parts. In these cases, it is best to do the second part shortly after the first part to keep the overall sense of the story in your head.

Finally, remember that you can look back to Part One whenever you need a reminder about the key reading skills you are applying in reading these texts.

Newsworthiness

12

Textbook extract
Skimming to preview
Understanding writer's purpose
Understanding main ideas
Understanding detail
Working out word meanings

PREPARING TO READ

answers page 134

1 Read the first paragraph of the text and then skim the rest for about 30 seconds, taking special notice of the headings. What is the main purpose of the text? (Tick one.)

a ______ to discuss the role of newspapers in today's world

b ______ to explain how journalists and editors select news stories

c ______ to describe different kinds of newspapers

NEWSWORTHINESS

paragraph

1 Journalists and editors select very carefully the stories they put into a newspaper. In the first place, millions of events occur around the world every day and not all can be fitted into the space available. In the second place, media organisations want to sell as many newspapers as possible, so they choose to report events they feel will interest most people. Journalists are therefore trained to make judgements about how newsworthy events are. Newsworthy events, in the main, are concerned with conflict, tragedy, crime, outstanding feats of achievement and the unusual.

Conflict

2 Many news stories are about conflict. An argument between workers and their employers about pay is an example of a newsworthy conflict. In contrast, an argument between individuals who are not well known is not usually considered newsworthy unless the dispute leads to violence. Even then, the violence would need to be extreme in order to be reported. A fist fight between arguing neighbours would not usually be newsworthy, but if one of them burnt down their neighbour's house the media would be likely to report it. The ultimate act of violent conflict is of course war between nations. However, even here, unless the home country is involved, the news reports of a war might only be brief.

Crime

3 People seem to enjoy reading about crime. Bombings, murders, armed robberies that involve large sums of money, and serious assaults attract readers. Notice that while crime can be newsworthy, violent crime is even more so. The unusual crime is also highly newsworthy. One type of unusual crime is when things go wrong for the criminal — for example, revealing their whereabouts by making calls on their mobile phones.

Tragedy

4 Events that kill and injure large numbers of people are considered newsworthy. Floods that leave people homeless, bushfires that roar through the countryside, and earthquakes all make 'good' news. People are fascinated and horrified by such events and will read about them avidly. The fascination is not just in the gloomy results of the events. These reports can make us feel lucky, because they did not happen to us. They can also make us feel good about being human when we read how people come to the aid of the victims, often at great risk to their own lives.

Outstanding feats

5 When a person does something that a large number of people admire or applaud, it is newsworthy. Feats of bravery and daring, and achievements of things never before attempted or accomplished are all considered worth reporting. The first humans in space, and later the first moon landing, were newsworthy because they were spectacular achievements. Everyday individuals are also newsworthy when they perform acts of heroism or kindness — the woman who enters a burning house to rescue her children, or the person who gives up a comfortable life to help starving or sick people. These events help to provide some sort of balance for the grim news that takes up so much media space.

Unusual events or human interest stories

6 There is usually space somewhere in a newspaper for stories which amaze or intrigue us, or simply make us feel good. A story about ducks being helped across the road by passing motorists on a busy freeway or about a very sick baby who beats incredible odds to survive are examples.

Other factors affecting news selection

7 News selection is also affected by other factors. One is currency — how recently the event happened. Old news is not good news and will not help to sell newspapers. This is one reason why newspapers compete fiercely to be the first with the news. Another condition that affects news selection is the proximity of the event — how close to home it occurred. Journalists consider murder in the local area to be more important news than a murder in a city 1000 kilometres away. The fame factor is also significant. Newspapers report almost every movement of movie stars and other celebrities, for example, the fact they have got married or divorced, but rarely report such events about the ordinary man or woman in the street.

(adapted from *Shaping the News*, by John D Fitzgerald, Harcourt Brace Jovanovich, Sydney, 1991.)

UNDERSTANDING THE TEXT

Read the whole text and answer the questions.

1 Most paragraphs begin with a topic sentence about newsworthiness. (A topic sentence states the main idea of a paragraph.) How does the writer develop the topic sentences? (Circle one.)

- **a** gives lists of examples
- **b** argues for or against the idea in the topic sentence
- **c** explains the idea in the topic sentence and gives examples

2 These sentences are missing from the text. Where would you add them? (Write the paragraph number and the last word of the sentence it would follow.)

- **a** It would be especially newsworthy if the conflict led to a strike by the workers. ________________
- **b** If a story can be read in one paper today, nobody will want to buy the competing papers to read the same story tomorrow. ________________________________
- **c** This is especially so if the crime happens locally. ____________________________
- **d** Other, less spectacular, events are also newsworthy — solo voyages across the world's oceans, for example. ________________________________
- **e** A single murder in a foreign country would not be reported at all unless the victim was a citizen of the home country. ________________________________

3 Complete the sentences.

- **a** In general, journalists choose stories that ____________________________
- **b** A conflict between two unknown people would only be reported if ________________
- **c** Detailed reports of wars in other countries are included if ____________________
- **d** Violent and ________________ crimes are most likely to be reported.
- **e** People read about tragic events because they ____________________________

  ____

  (give two reasons)
- **f** One kind of story that balances the bad news is ____________________________

4 Find a word that means the same as these words in the following paragraphs.

a extraordinary acts (para 1, 5) ____________

b most extreme (para 2) ____________

c with great interest (para 4) ____________

d praise (para 5) ____________

e very unpleasant (para 5) ____________

f involve and interest (para 6) ____________

RESPONDING TO THE TEXT

1 Write one or two paragraphs about newsworthiness suitable for a research report on the media. You should try to include all the main factors explained in the text, and at least some examples. (These could be from the text or based on your own experiences.)

2 Do *we* control what we read or do journalists? Write a few sentences about what *you* think. (Use the space below or your own paper.)

Never say die

13

Feature article extract
Predicting
Skimming to preview
Working out word meanings
Understanding detail
Understanding complex sentences

PREPARING TO READ

answers page 134

1 Read the introduction to the text (in **bold**). Then tick the information you expect to find in the article.

______ Stories of people who have survived life-threatening situations.

______ Medical explanations of how the body reacts in these situations.

______ Stories about how some survivors sell their stories for a lot of money.

______ Instructions about how to get out of dangerous situations.

2 Now quickly skim the whole extract. Which information above *does* it contain?

____

____

NEVER SAY DIE

paragraph

Entombed, frozen, burnt, besieged — how is it that some people, in the face of death, become almost superhuman in their will to live? *Nikki Barrowclough* looks at the miraculous human capacity to survive. **intro**

Val Plumwood had the feeling she was being watched. It was late afternoon and she was paddling alone in a small canoe through the magnificent paperbark wetlands of Kakadu in search of an Aboriginal rock site. Wet season rain squalls had reduced the day to gloom, and the setting had begun to seem a little menacing. **1**

Without warning, a crocodile appeared midstream, directly in front of her. Plumwood saw she was going to pass close to the creature but was totally unprepared for what happened next. The crocodile lunged at the canoe, attacking it with a series of huge blows from its tail, then pursued her as she paddled furiously away. **2**

Plumwood made for the steep mud slope at the side of the channel, heading for a paperbark tree whose branches hung low over the water. Standing up in the canoe, she readied herself to leap. But before her foot touched the first branch, she had a 'blurred, incredulous vision of great-toothed jaws bursting from the water', then she was seized in the groin 'in a red-hot pincer grip' and whirled into the darkness below. **3**

Few people have survived a crocodile's death roll. Plumwood survived three of them and later wrote about the experiences in the magazine *Quadrant*. It makes for compelling reading. At one stage, when her head broke the surface after the second death roll, Plumwood grabbed the thick branch of a tree growing in the water. The crocodile was still holding her between the legs but, as the creature's jaws relaxed, she used the branch to pull herself free. Then as she began her desperate climb into the branches, the crocodile again propelled itself from the water, seized her around the upper left thigh and wrenched her back down for the third time. **4**

Despite what by now were serious injuries, Plumwood felt only a 'hot sensation' from the creature's jaws. Incredibly, she still didn't drown. In an act of almost unimaginable courage and presence of mind, she rammed her thumbs into two unresisting holes — probably the creature's ears — and after heaving herself from the crocodile's jaws, flung herself at the mud bank, scrabbling her way up it. As her grip failed and she began sliding back towards the bottom — and the waiting crocodile — she grabbed a tuft of grass and hung onto it for dear life. When the tuft began to give away, she pushed her fingers into the mud and managed to haul herself, finally, to the top. **5**

Severely injured and covered in blood, her left thigh hanging open with bits of fat, tendon and muscle showing, Plumwood dragged herself, staggering and frequently passing out, through the driving rain towards where she knew there was a ranger's headquarters — a journey which took her several hours. By now she was in a lot of pain, 'but it was a sort of shocked, numbed pain', she says. She crawled the final distance to the edge of a swamp near the ranger station, where she was found much later, semi-conscious. It was only after her rescuers put her on a stretcher that the pain really hit her in full. **6**

Almost 16 years later, the attack remains as vivid in her memory as ever. Says Plumwood: 'It seemed as if I had suddenly been catapulted into this world where I was food for something else.' Plumwood has lost some of the function in her left thigh, and has occasional problems walking. But she has never forgotten the fighting spirit she discovered she possessed as she struggled to escape, nor the speed of her thought processes during the attack. **7**

Time and again we hear of men and women demonstrating an almost superhuman will to live in the most horrendous circumstances. Like Plumwood, they find themselves so focused on survival that it overrides everything else, including fear, pain and injury. They swim through shark-infested waters, get buried in blizzards or vanish in remote areas, then emerge, battered and wounded, long after being given up for dead. Their survival stories highlight the great paradox of the human body: while something as simple as falling and hitting your head on the pavement can kill you, you can also endure the most extreme conditions. **8**

(from *Sydney Morning Herald*, Good Weekend, 12 May 2001, pp 16–17)

UNDERSTANDING THE TEXT

Now read the whole text carefully.

1 Circle True or False.

a Val Plumwood felt a little uncomfortable before she saw the crocodile. True / False

b When Val first saw the crocodile, she expected it to attack her. True / False

c Val did not see the crocodile attacking her the first time. True / False

d The crocodile made two attacks on the lower half of Val's body. True / False

e Val was in very great pain throughout the attack. True / False

f The crocodile relaxed its grip on Val when she pushed her thumbs into its ears. True / False

g Val slipped down the mud bank once before making it to the top. True / False

h Val did not know where she was. True / False

i Val remembers the strange feeling that she had become food for another creature. True / False

j The writer believes that only a few people can use their will to survive to make them forget fear, pain and injury. True / False

2 Answer the following questions.

a Why was Val Plumwood on the river? ______________________________

b How did Val try to escape the crocodile the first time? ______________________________

c What does a 'death roll' mean? ______________________________

d How did Val get to the ranger station? ______________________________

e Why are some parts of the text in inverted commas? ______________________________

3 Find these words, and read the surrounding text. Then underline the words that seem closest in meaning based on the context and your own knowledge of the word

a	**menacing** (para 1)	threatening	annoying
b	**lunged** (para 2)	moved forward suddenly	swam towards
c	**furiously** (para 2)	in anger	with great energy and speed
d	**incredulous** (para 3)	not wanting to believe	not able to be believed
e	**wrenched** (para 4)	pushed with force	pulled with force
f	**presence of mind** (para 5)	quick thinking	cleverness
g	**scrabbling** (para 5)	climbing	scratching and scraping
h	**tuft** (para 5)	bank of long grass	a clump of short grass
i	**endure** (para 8)	put up with for a long time	fight back
j	**paradox** (para 8)	extraordinary achievement or miracle	idea/situation hard to understand because it contains opposing facts

4 The paragraph below from the article has had all the punctuation taken out. Read the paragraph through and put capital letters, full stops, commas and other punctuation marks where needed to make the paragraph make sense. (To do this you have to read carefully and actively.) Then check your work against paragraph 5 on page 57.

In a few spots there is more than one way to punctuate, but generally your punctuation should match Nikki Barrowclough's. It is worth noting how well the journalist has used punctuation to help tell the story in a clear and engaging way.

> despite what by now were serious injuries Plumwood felt only a hot sensation from the creature's jaws incredibly she still didn't drown in an act of almost unimaginable courage and presence of mind she rammed her thumbs into two unresisting holes probably the creature's ears and after heaving herself from the crocodile's jaws flung herself at the mud bank scrabbling her way up it as her grip failed and she began sliding back towards the bottom and the waiting crocodile she grabbed a tuft of grass and hung onto it for dear life when the tuft began to give away she pushed her fingers into the mud and managed to haul herself finally to the top

RESPONDING TO THE TEXT

Write down or tell another person what you found the most amazing part of the story, and why. (Use your own paper.)

SPOTLIGHT ON LANGUAGE

- The writer uses many powerful verbs to describe the action that takes place. For example, *lunged* (para 2), *bursting* (para 3). Can you find others?
- An excellent way to expand your vocabulary is to take a few minutes after reading good, interesting texts to look back at new words and the ways they are used. You could then write these words somewhere for use in your own writing, making a kind of 'personal dictionary'.

Look through *Never Say Die* now and underline the words that were new for you, or words which were used in new ways. If you wish, write the words in your personal dictionary, and add notes about their meanings or usage.

Contact — Part One

Novel extract
Predicting
Understanding text organisation
Working out word meanings
Understanding imagery
Inferring

PREPARING TO READ

answers page 135

Read the first two paragraphs of the story *only* and answer the questions.

1 What is the woman in the story doing? ______________________________

2 How does she feel and why? ______________________________

3 Do you think the next few pages will mainly (tick one)

a ______ narrate what happens?

b ______ discuss the woman's background?

c ______ explain why the woman is in this situation?

Give your reasons.

____

____

4 Now read the whole text and check your prediction.

CONTACT
By Penny Hall
Part One

Mahla

paragraph

1 She'd slowed the craft as much as she dared. Her eyes flicked back and forth, from the control panel to the mountainous terrain below. Where, oh where could she land this thing in such bleak, awful territory?

2 The airspeed indicator shrilled its 'too slow' warning. Hastily, she accelerated until there was only the unbroken shush of the wind on the canopy and the steady hum of the engine. Normally she loved these sounds, but right now they were an unnerving reminder of aloneness and danger. She glanced quickly over her shoulder. The snow-filled clouds were building up rapidly over the mountains behind her, and she knew she hadn't a hope of outrunning them.

The narrow valley down which she was flying swung east and widened. She could 3
safely set down here but there was nothing, not even a solitary tree, to protect the craft from the snow which she knew was to come.

Now the valley veered north. Before her lay a vast stretch of winter-bare trees and 4
beyond them she could see not just a single farm house, but a whole town.

'Go, Mahla,' she breathed out loud. 5

The craft bucked as a wraith-finger of cloud, a forerunner of the terrifying body massed 6
behind, coiled over its transparent canopy.

For one wild moment, Mahla considered flying through the forest. No, she would have 7
to go round. She grinned wryly to herself as she simultaneously banked the craft and increased the speed. Seconds ago she'd been praying for the protection of just one decent-sized tree, and now there were hundreds, maybe thousands, of the damned things between her and safety. She had to go round them while the storm swept over and through them.

The first snowflakes dusted the skin of the capsule as she raced down the length of the 8
forest. The swirling winds on the outer edges of the storm rocked the lightweight craft, forcing her to decrease speed slightly, to let it settle closer to the ground.

She'd come to the end of the forest and now she had to steer across the path of the 9
storm. The town lay before her. It seemed to be made up of huge houses enclosed by high timber fences that sealed them completely from outsiders. There was no movement on what little she could see of the streets through the thickening storm, but threads of grey smoke from the chimneys bent to the wind.

I'd much rather be in front of a fire inside a nice solid house too, she thought, as she 10
tried to peer though the insubstantial greyness rapidly masking the town.

Should she risk taking the craft into the town? Why not? No one in their right mind 11
would be out in this weather and the high fences would give some protection from the wind. If she left the craft outside the town, at best it would be flipped over and at worst it would be blown away.

She remembered her flying instructor saying that some remote places might still use 12
overhead powerlines. She couldn't see any so that meant one less hazard in her path.

She slowed to the merest creep. The electronic warning screamed again, and she 13
swore at the sound for intruding on her concentration.

(Angus and Robertson, HarperCollins, Sydney, 1993, pp 1–3)

UNDERSTANDING THE TEXT

1 In which order do these events occur? Number them 1–6.

______ Snow fell on the plane.

______ She saw a town in the valley.

______ She saw chimney smoke.

______ She slowed the aircraft because of the mountains.

______ Snowclouds first touched the plane.

______ She flew around the forest.

2 The writer uses words and expressions to paint a picture in our minds of the main action. Through most of the text, do you think the writer 'paints a picture' of someone (circle one)

a being chased?

b playing a dangerous game?

c fighting an opponent?

Write down the words and expressions that paint this picture.

____

____

3 In paragraph 6, the writer describes the first snowcloud.

a Look up the word 'wraith' in your dictionary and write it down.

____

b What kind of picture of the snowclouds do you have in your mind.

____

c Which words especially paint this picture?

____

4 Find the words (**a–j**) in the text and re-read the paragraph. Circle the word or expression which is closest to the meaning of each word.

a	**terrain** (para 1)	climate	landform	hilly land
b	**bleak** (para 1)	dull and boring	very cold	bare and windswept
c	**canopy** (para 2/6)	part of the plane over the pilot's head	pilot's headgear	
d	**unnerving** (para 2)	unhappy	disturbing	nervous

e	**veered** (para 4)	turned	faced	went
f	**wryly** (para 7)	with bitter amusement	with pleasure	with pain
g	**insubstantial** (para 10)	airy and light	heavy and thick	like liquid
h	**remote** (para 12)	old-fashioned	distant and isolated	high country
i	**merest** (para 13)	nothing less than	nothing more than	slowest
j	**intruding on** (para 13)	interrupting	stopping	irritating

5 On the basis of what you have read so far, what do you think about (circle one)

a the time setting of the story? present past future

Give reasons for your answer.

____

____

b the town? friendly unfriendly evil

Give reasons for your answer.

____

____

c Mahla and the people in the town very alike very different

Give reasons for your answer.

____

____

RESPONDING TO THE TEXT

How interested are you in reading the next part of the text (see following chapter)? Why or why not? (Use your own paper.)

Contact — Part Two

15

Novel extract
Predicting
Understanding main ideas
Understanding detail
Working out word meanings

PREPARING TO READ

answers page 135

1 Based on what you have read in Part 1 in the previous chapter (and without looking at the text which follows) do you predict that Mahla will (tick as many as you like):

______ land the plane with difficulty?

______ land the plane with ease?

______ crash the plane?

______ be injured while landing the plane?

______ meet someone who helps her?

______ find herself completely alone?

Now read the whole text carefully.

CONTACT

By Penny Hall **paragraph**

Part Two

Now it was almost dark. It wasn't the friendly, multi-layered tones of the night blackness, but the suffocating monotone of the stuff of nightmares. The slow speed meant her control of the craft was minimal. It dipped and swayed with every little swirl and eddy of the wind, and still the warning screamed. **1**

In desperation, she turned into a street running at right angles to the storm. There were raised footpaths on either side and a deep channel down the middle. It was impossible to steer the craft over the wind-funnel of the channel and she forced it up onto the footpath where she could use the fence as a windbreak and a line of sight. **2**

She couldn't think with that screaming in her ears. She accelerated viciously, and the craft shot forward. Almost instantly, the alarm cut out, leaving the sound of the air on the hull and the purr of the engine. **3**

A freak gust of wind suddenly cleared the mist before her. The street led straight through the town and out the other side. She'd have to stop where she was and take a chance on being able to get people from one of the houses to let her leave the craft in a sheltered corner of their yard. **4**

A gateway was coming up, just a few metres ahead. She slammed on the brake 5
and the craft stalled and sank to the ground, right in front of the gates. She slid the canopy backwards and breathed in deeply, gasping at the shock of the cold moist air filling her lungs and settling on her face and bare arms.

The wind was growing stronger, pinning her to the seat. She must undo the harness, 6
get out of the craft and force open those dauntingly solid gates. She could do it. Of course she could do it. She'd come this far, hadn't she?

Undoing the harness was easy. Standing and stepping out of the craft was not so 7
easy, but she did it. She leant into the wind, straining towards the gates. Did they open towards or away from her? Would she have the strength to open those huge structures against the wind or would they sweep outwards, throwing her and her craft across the street?

It was madness to stand here, lashed by the wind, shivering in the cold. She took one 8
step forward. The enormous panels before her flexed, bulged and, with the agonised shriek of wood tearing away from metal, burst open.

There was nothing she could do. One panel caught her down the length of the body 9
and flicked her away with the ease of a bat striking a ball. Her scream was lost in the insane howling of the wind and the fearful grinding of shredding fibreglass as the other panel connected with the craft.

She was still upright when she hit the fence on the far side of the road. Her body was 10
a fireball of agony and a tiny part of her brain asked, 'How can one body hurt this much?', before she dropped to the ground and lost consciousness.

(Angus and Robertson, HarperCollins Sydney, 1993, pp 3–5)

UNDERSTANDING THE TEXT

1 Answer these questions.

a How does Mahla usually feel about the dark? ______________________

b How does she feel about the dark on this night? ______________________

c Why did Mahla want to go faster? ______________________

d What was the *screaming in her ears* (para 3)? (Look back at Part One if you are not sure.)

____

e What is unusual about the town streets?

____

f Why did Mahla force the plane onto the footpath (give two reasons)?

____

g What was the most difficult part of getting out of the craft?

____

h Who or what opened the gates?

____

i What caused the 'fearful grinding' noise (para 9)?

____

j Describe exactly what happened to Mahla when the gates opened.

____

____

2 Much of the meaning of the text depends on understanding where Mahla was. Do a simple drawing (lines and stick figures are enough) to show the streets, the footpaths, the gates, and Mahla and her aircraft just before the gates opened. Use your own paper.

3 Find a word in the text that means:

a circular, whirling movement (para 1) ____________

b state of hopelessness (para 2) ____________

c highly unusual (para 4) ____________

d frighteningly (para 6) ____________

e whipped (para 8) ____________

f bended (para 8) ____________

g swelled (para 8) ____________

RESPONDING TO THE TEXT

The two parts of *Contact* you have read are from the first chapter of the book. A first chapter often leaves us with many questions. The writer does not tell us exactly what it is going on or why. They do this to engage our interest — to make us ask questions about what is going on.

What questions are in your mind now about this story? What ideas do you have about how the story might develop? Write down your questions and ideas on your own paper.

SPOTLIGHT ON LANGUAGE

- The writer uses many words and expressions to describe the sounds of the action. Look back over Parts One and Two of *Contact* and underline all 'sound' words and expressions that you can find. Write them in two lists — one for sounds which are likely to have a positive effect on the hearer and the other for sounds which are likely to have a negative effect. (Use your own paper.)
- The story includes questions in both text extracts (Part One, para 11; and Part Two, paras 6 and 7). Who is asking the questions, and of whom? How do they help to make the story interesting? (Use the space below or your own paper.)

Cannibalism in animals

16

Fact sheet
Skimming to preview
Understanding main ideas
Understanding text organisation
Understanding detail
Understanding complex sentences
Working out word meanings

PREPARING TO READ

answers page 136

1 Read the headings from the text, *Cannibalism*, and think about the kind of information you might find in each section:

- *What is cannibalism?*
- *Why do animals become cannibals?*
- *The benefits of cannibalism*
- *Environmental pressures*
- *Infanticide*

2 Now skim the text for 30 seconds and see if your ideas were correct.

CANNIBALISM IN ANIMALS

paragraph

What is cannibalism?

The word cannibalism is derived from the name of an island race called the Canibales. This war-like tribe had the unpleasant habit of feasting on their enemies killed or captured in battle. The name has since been applied to any animal which eats others of its own species. **1**

There are basically two kinds of cannibals: active cannibals and passive cannibals. An active cannibal actually hunts and kills others of its own kind, before eating them. A passive cannibal simply feeds on dead members of its own species, which it may happen upon. Active cannibalism may also take various forms. In some species, for example, it occurs only between animals of one generation (fratricide), while among others it is most common between adults and their offspring (kronism). **2**

Why do animals become cannibals?

In general, cannibalism can be regarded as a particular form of feeding behaviour where a predatory species also preys upon — or simply eats — animals of its own kind. Perhaps surprisingly, however, cannibalism is often not the result of a predator's efficiency, but quite the reverse. Few of the top flesh-eaters, such as wolves and tigers, ever eat those of their own kind. And even those that do, like the spotted hyena, are usually passive cannibals. Instead, cannibalism is more prevalent among lower animals, such as praying mantises or ladybird larvae, when it is often the result of the animal lacking the ability to distinguish between its relatives and its prey. **3**

The benefits of cannibalism

Cannibalism may be purely destructive, but it can, in fact, be quite beneficial. Clearly, a voraciously cannibalistic species would rapidly eat itself out of existence. But when cannibalistic activity occurs as a response to overcrowding, for example, it can actually increase a species' chance of survival. For, if a population were to rise too rapidly without restraint, it could completely eliminate its own food supply. During a harsh winter or drought, when food is scarce, it is clearly to a species' advantage for at least some of the population to remain well fed and healthy — even at the expense of other companions. **4**

Among species that produce many offspring, the cannibalism of siblings can also help ensure that enough young develop into adults, and so continue the species. In species such as the spadefoot tadpole and flour beetle, for example, cannibalism appears to be an inherited trait. **5**

Environmental pressures

Some non-cannibalistic animals can become cannibals when faced with certain environmental conditions. Mice and rats, for example, may turn cannibal when their colony population rises rapidly, and their naturally high reproductive rate results in a high mortality of young. The dead offspring may then be cannibalised by the hungry and highly stressed survivors. This behaviour has most often been observed in animals kept under unnaturally cramped conditions in captivity — but there is also evidence of it occurring in the wild under similar conditions. **6**

Infanticide

Of the higher mammals, the lion seems to show the most definite cannibalistic tendencies. There have been many reports of male lions killing and then sometimes eating young cubs. In almost all cases, however, the male lion is not prompted to kill the cubs through hunger, or even population pressure, but through a need to safeguard his own offspring. In most cases, moreover, the young are killed but not eaten. The killing is best described as infanticide (the killing of young) rather than cannibalism. This infanticide is an effective, if bloody way to ensure that a male's own offspring survive at the expense of his rivals. This extreme behaviour is linked to the fact that a female lion reproduces quite slowly, usually coming into season again after her cubs have become independent. Also the male has a breeding period of only around three years. So when he secures a pride of breeding females, time is of the essence. By killing any cubs and young lions present, he both encourages the females to come into season and eliminates the chance of any rivalry against offspring he later fathers. The males of several species of the higher primates (for example, baboons) practise infanticide in the same way. **7**

(from *Wildlife Factfile*, International Masters Publishers Australia P/L, Group 8 Animal Behaviour, Card 14)

UNDERSTANDING THE TEXT

1 Now read the text fully. Complete this chart, based on information in 'What is cannibalism?'

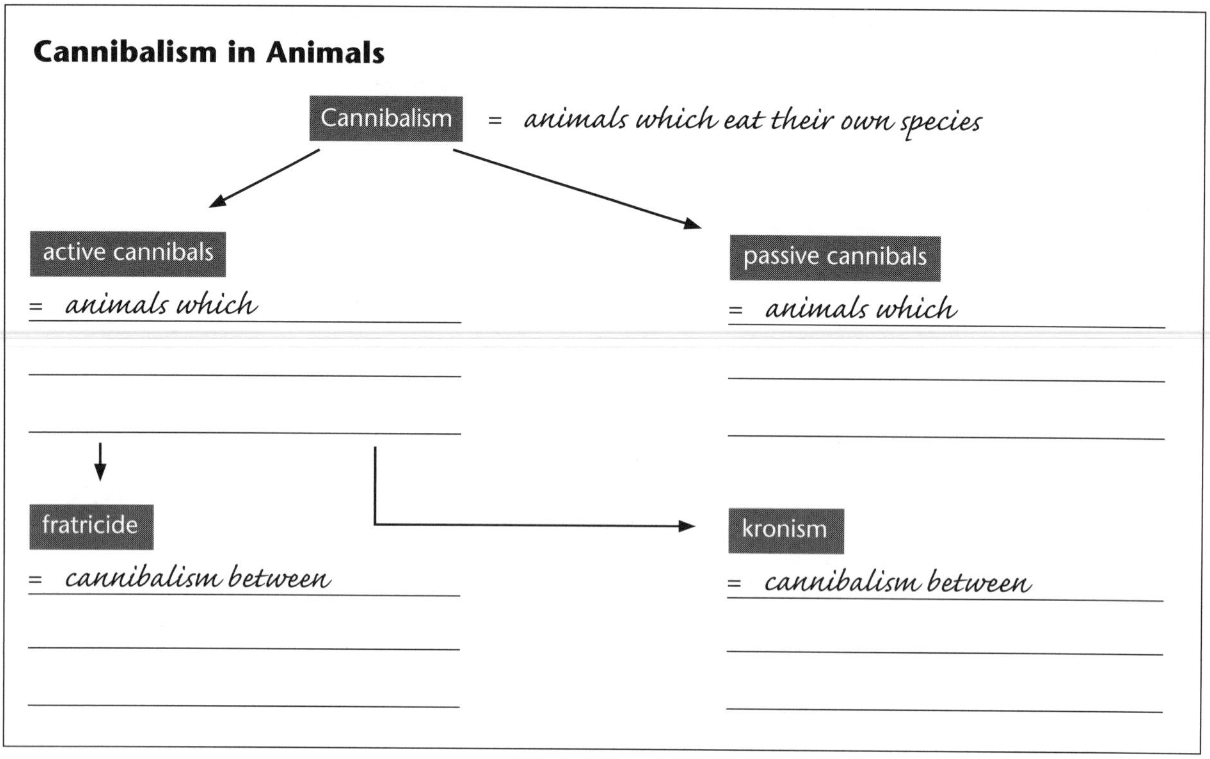

2 Answer the questions or complete the sentences.

a Most cannibalism occurs amongst species which are skillful predators. True or false? ____________

b Top flesh eaters generally only eat dead members of their own species. True or false? ____________

c Cannibalism can benefit a species in times of overcrowding by ________________________

d When there is not much food, it is better to have a small number of well fed animals.

True or false? ____________

e Cannibalism is never inherited — it is always an adaptation to the environment.

True or false? ____________

f Male lions kill young cubs to ____

g This practice is called ____________________, not cannibalism, because ________________

____

h What two factors in the reproductive cycle of lions influence the male lion's behaviour?

____

____

3 Find the words (**a–h**) in the text, and use the context to work out their meanings. Choose words with similar meanings from the list below, and write them in the spaces.

widespread

greedily, quickly, or in great quantities

death rate

control or restriction

characteristic

extremely important

in addition

while damaging

a prevalent (para 3) ______________________________

b voraciously (para 4) ______________________________

c restraint (para 4) ______________________________

d at the expense of (para 4/8) ______________________________

e trait (para 5) ______________________________

f mortality (para 6) ______________________________

g moreover (para 7) ______________________________

h of the essence (para 7) ______________________________

RESPONDING TO THE TEXT

Imagine that someone says to you that cannibalism shows that a species is particularly savage and cruel. What would you say to them, based on what you know after reading this text? Write down your answer. (Use your own paper.)

SPOTLIGHT ON LANGUAGE

Cannibalism, cannibal, cannibalistic, cannibalise are all words formed from the base word *cannibal.* *Predatory, prey, predator* are all words formed from the base word *prey.*

Underline these words where they occur in the text, and note what part of speech each is (e.g. noun, verb, adjective, adverb).

Pocket money tops $50

17

Newspaper report
Scanning
Understanding charts
Reading critically
Inferring
Understanding detail

PREPARING TO READ

answers page 136

Read *only* the headline and subheadline of the newspaper article opposite and answer these questions.

1 What does the headline tell you about pocket money and 10–14 year olds?

____

2 How much pocket money do you think you *should* get? ______________

3 Is this more or less than you *do* get? ______________

UNDERSTANDING THE TEXT

1 Scan the table on the opposite page to find the answers to these questions. (Don't read the article yet.)

a How many children of 14–15 years are getting no pocket money? ______________

b What is the most common amount given to 14–15 year olds (*including* none at all)? ______________

c How many 10–11 year olds are getting $50 or more? ______________

d How many 14–15 year olds are getting $50 or more? ______________

e What is the most common amount of pocket money for most children (*including* none at all)? ______

f Which is the larger group — children who get pocket money or children who don't?

____

2 **a** Based *only* on information in the chart, how accurate is the headline?

____

b Why do think the headline was written as it was?

____

Now read the article.

Pocket Money Tops $50

That's the rate for many kids at 14 — and even 10 — says survey.

By Johanna Leggatt

1 Children as young as 10 are receiving more than $50 a week in pocket money as parents give in to their demands.

2 If it's not a trip to the aquarium, it's the zoo. If it's not the latest PlayStation games, it is something equally damaging to the wallet.

3 A recent Youth Scan survey by Quantum Market Research showed many kids between the ages of 10 and 11 receive from $1 to $10 weekly pocket money.

4 But researcher David Chalke said he was stunned to find one 10-year-old who ticked the '$50 and over' box.

5 'It certainly seems that kids are getting more money off parents and they're also doing outside jobs to get even more,' he said.

6 The Quantum survey found that most 14 and 15 year olds getting pocket money were given between $10 and $20 a week — but 5% of 14 to 15 year olds receive more than $50 a week.

7 At the other end of the spectrum are the more than 40% of parents who said they didn't give their children any pocket money.

8 'It's not something I think I can give my children fairly,' said Maureen Thompson, mother of 12-year-old twins Bethany and Kirraly. 'One is really good at saving and the other isn't, so one would constantly have money and the other wouldn't.'

9 Paul Jackson, father of Monisha, 9, and Zoe, 7, gives his daughters between $5 and $20 a week depending on what they need.

10 'I have no problem with it because I think they need to learn the value of money and how far it goes,' he said. 'When the money is gone it's gone, and they learn pretty quickly not to spend it in the first few minutes.'

11 Clinical psychologist Janet Milne, who works with children, said while she believed pocket money was a good idea, it was important for parents not to 'buy kids everything.'

12 'But I don't think parents should go the other way either and not give their kids anything consumer-driven, because that puts them on the outside at school.'

HOW MUCH CHILDREN ARE BEING PAID

	10–17 years	10–11 years	12–13 years	14–15 years	16–17 years
No pocket money	46%	43%	45%	44%	58%
Less than $1	1%	1%	0	1%	0
$1 to $9.99	20%	41%	26%	11%	3%
$10 to $19.99	16%	12%	17%	19%	12%
$20 to $29.99	10%	2%	9%	14%	13%
$30 to $39.99	2%	0	1%	3%	3%
$40 to $49.99	2%	0	1%	3%	3%
$50 plus	3%	1%	1%	5%	8%

Source: Youth Scan survey by Quantum Market Research (*Sun-Herald*, 20 October 2002, p. 36)

3 Answer these questions.

a Which company conducted the survey? ______________________

b How many people are quoted in the article? ______________________

c The researcher says that he was stunned to find one 10-year-old respondent who ticked the '$50 and over' box? Look at the chart and work out how many 10–11 year olds were surveyed.

____

d Think back to your answer to **2** above. Can you add anything to that statement now?

____

e Does Maureen Thompson give her children pocket money? ______________________

Why/why not? ______________________

f Does Paul Jackson give his children pocket money? ______________________

Why/why not? ______________________

g Why is Janet Milne's opinion given? ______________________

h What is Janet Milne's opinion (in your own words)? ______________________

4 When reading reports of research, it is important to think about how the results might have been obtained, and what this means for how you interpret the results.

a Tick the boxes to show if/how the information is given in the article. (The first one has been done for you.)

Information about research method	Stated explicitly (directly)	Can be inferred (worked out)	Not stated explicitly or able to be inferred
What question/questions were asked	—	√	—
How the information was obtained (e.g. written survey, interview)			
How many children were surveyed			
Where children lived (e.g. city, country)			

b Can you think of one way that this kind of information could affect the way we interpret the results?

____

RESPONDING TO THE TEXT

Write a short text putting forward the reasons for and against pocket money. (Use your own paper.)

How science began to solve crimes

18

Information book extract

Skimming to preview
Understanding text organisation
Understanding main ideas
Understanding detail
Working out word meanings

PREPARING TO READ

answers page 137

Read the first and last paragraphs of the text on page 77, and quickly skim the other paragraphs. Then turn back to this page and write down as many words as you can remember from the text.

____

____

UNDERSTANDING THE TEXT

Now read the text fully and answer the following questions.

1 To understand the text, the reader needs to follow the time sequence. Write *during, after,* or *before* in the spaces below.

a Bertillion's method of detection was introduced ________________ the 16th century.

b Fingerprinting was a method that was introduced ________________ anthropometry.

c Torturing was a method used ________________ the 16th century.

d Detectives started paying attention to clues ________________ the 1800s.

e People often believed it was wrong to try to solve crimes ________________ the 17th century.

2 Tick the sentence that best sums up the main idea of the whole text.

a ______ Looking for clues and using scientific systems to solve crimes is quite a recent development.

b ______ In the 16th century forensic science did not exist.

c ______ There are now many different kinds of forensic science used to solve crimes.

d ______ The people who work to solve crimes are a dedicated group of people.

3 Often little words make a big difference to the meaning. Read the text closely and then choose one answer to complete each sentence below.

a In the 16th century, criminal investigation meant

______ only looking for suspects. ______ mainly looking for suspects.

b Sixteenth century officials looked for

______ a person to blame. ______ the person who committed the crime.

c Before forensic science could develop, people had to accept that

______ it was a good idea to use thought and reasoning to solve crime.

______ torturing was not the best way to solve crime.

d Forensic science was not really accepted until

______ the 1700s. ______ the 1800s.

e Bertillion's system was

______ simple in every way. ______ a simple idea but complex in practice.

f Bertillion's system looked at

______ the measurements of the head and fingers first.

______ the measurements of the head and fingers only.

g In general when new methods of crime detection are introduced, people accept them

______ slowly ______ quickly.

4 Find these words in the text. Use the context to give another word or words for each.

a scapegoat (para 2) ____________________

b forensic science (para 3) ____________________

b anthropometry (para 5) ____________________

d misidentification (para 6) ____________________

e cumbersome (para 8) ____________________

f skeptics (para 9) ____________________

RESPONDING TO THE TEXT

Write down three topics you would like to know more about after reading this text.

SPOTLIGHT ON LANGUAGE

In information texts, writers make frequent use of linking words to show how the ideas in one sentence connect with the ideas in the next. Go through the text and underline these linking words: *Sometimes ..., Other times ..., Of course ... , In fact ..., On one occasion ..., twelve months earlier ..., But even so ..., In fact ... .*

HOW SCIENCE BEGAN TO SOLVE CRIMES

paragraph

by Anita Larsen

In the 16th century, there were no detectives like the ones we know of today. Criminal investigation meant little more than looking for suspects, with almost no attempt made to find clues. Sometimes officials simply walked away from puzzling crimes — they didn't even try to solve them. **1**

Other times, officials found a scapegoat, a person who might be innocent but who could be accused and punished anyway. The point was to discover *a* culprit rather than *the* culprit; at least this satisfied society that the crime had not gone unpunished. **2**

Standard 16th-century procedure was torturing people until they confessed their guilt. Of course, torture was highly effective in producing a speedy confession. This had gone on for hundreds of years, and was thought to be the best way to solve a crime. In fact, before the 17th century, great numbers of people believed it was wrong to even try solving crimes by using thought and reasoning. That had to change before forensic science, the science of crime solution, could begin to develop. **3**

Once people began to accept the notion that logic was valuable in crime-solving, the field of forensic science began to grow — but slowly. It finally came into its own in the 1800s. That was when authorities began to listen carefully to the information being shouted by the clues left at a crime scene. **4**

The next step forward was taken when detectives realised that much more could be learned from clues if they used new systems to help in analysing them. One of the earliest systems was Alphonse Bertillion's 'anthropometry.' **5**

What Bertillion did was simple enough. He took eleven measurements of arrested criminals. The most important of these measurements were the length and width of the criminal's head, middle fingers, and the little finger of the left hand. The odds of misidentification were relatively small since the odds of two people having identical measurements in these four areas are 276 to 1. The odds against misidentification rose to almost 4,000,000 to 1 when seven other measurements were applied. Then Bertillion filed all this data on cards. Each card carried two photos of the person and details of previous arrest records. **6**

Bertillion's system helped solve many crimes by identifying the living, and it provided another benefit, too — identifying the dead. On one occasion a police colleague of Bertillion's, an inspector, asked him to identify a corpse that had been shot several months earlier. The inspector was trying to have some fun by embarrassing the new identification method, but Bertillion believed in his system so firmly that he accepted the challenge. **7**

Bertillion's system might have been competent, but it was cumbersome. Fortunately, a more easily managable means of identification was soon discovered — fingerprints. Fingerprints were easier to obtain than all the measurements required by Bertillion's method. They were also easier to keep track of and use. **8**

But even so, the new fingerprint system faced an uphill battle to convince the skeptics. In fact, few advances in forensic science have won acceptance easily. The true cases that follow show how some of the many branches of the forensic sciences developed and grew. They are evidence of the dedication and triumph of forensic scientists, who work in crime labs to help detectives solve seemingly unsolvable crimes. **9**

(from *True crimes and how they were solved*, Scholastic Inc, New York, 1993, pp 1–3)

Life on the edge

19

Feature article extract

Skimming to preview • Inferring
Understanding humour • Understanding main idea
Understanding language techniques

PREPARING TO READ

answers page 137

1 The following text is an extract from a larger feature article on the growth of extreme sports. Skim the text for 30 seconds. What is this extract's main purpose? (Circle one.)

a ______ to tell the reader what you need to do to learn sky-diving

b ______ to explain the different kinds of extreme sports you can do

c ______ to tell the reader what the sky-diving experience is like

Life On The Edge

Paragraph

Why do seemingly sane, mature people feel the need to jump out of planes, feed sharks by hand or cycle down a cliff? Do we need danger? *Deirdre Macken* investigates the growth and psychology of extreme sports. **intro**

This is insane. Not cool insane, not wow insane. This is just crazy. The door of the plane has just opened. At 13,500 feet. Whipping wind, sucking air pressure and roaring engine. An experienced parachutist walks to the door. Looks. And jumps. Head first, out the door. Now there are two tandem jumpers left. **1**

Joanne, a tourist from England, crouches towards the door strapped to the chest of a tandem master. It's her second jump. Grey-faced, she glances down. The M5 freeway is taking trucks to town. Ships are cruising out of Wollongong. The Nepean Dam is emptying. But she doesn't have time to notice all this. They too are gone. Head first. Out the door. Gone. Like in the movies. Or a nightmare. Now there's only one tandem jump to go. A novice. No. No. This is insane. It should be said. Try to tell Craig Field, the tandem master, this can't be done. But he's already walking to the door. He has momentum. Lift your legs off the ground, he says. Put your head back, arms crossed over your chest. The classic sacrifice pose. This is insane! It should be said. In time. To stop. Go back. To the front of the plane. Back to the ground. To the womb maybe. **2**

Extreme sports. Death-defying experiences. They used to be confined to B-grade movies, television commercials and the lives of wacky adventurers in tough boots and strange hats. Now they belong to everyone's weekend. Jumping out of planes, swimming with sharks, canyoning, white-water rafting, bungy jumping, boulder hopping, mountain biking, rock climbing … the dare has been declared. Leave behind the speed limits, the smoke-free zones, tight deadlines, the low-fat shopping list, the SPF-15 routine and yell in the face of life. There are no excuses now. Just pick up the phone. **3**

Midweek at the skydiving centre is quiet. On weekends there are some 20 flights a day. Two hundred people lifted. And dropped. The vast majority are tandems. Ninety-eight per cent first-timers. Co-director Phil Onis (12,234 jumps) says it takes most people one year from when they decide to do a jump to when they jump. Few come back for a second jump. Why, Phil? **4**

Steve Dines, a photographer at the centre, says the only thing that surprises him about tandem skydiving is the fact that people arrive here, chat with a tandem master for five minutes and then put their lives in that guy's hands. 'Sorta weird,' he says. Glance at tandem master. Craig. Been chatting with him 10 minutes. Seems like family already. Besides, he's done almost 6,000 jumps. Sounds good. Think again. Maybe he's about to run out of odds. What are the odds? No-one will say. And how's he feeling today, anyway? Wish he'd take the dark glasses off. **5**

The plane is noisy. It rises fast. Ear-popping fast. This is the quietest time for jumpers. Can't talk, can't hear. The tandem masters point out the window to attractive views. Intent on distracting us. Maybe they can sense the mounting fear. Or smell it. A few last questions. Can you breathe on the way down? Some people can't, says Craig, because they've forgotten to take a breath, so just scream, then you'll know you're breathing. A final admission. I didn't handle the Space Probe at Wonderland very well. Don't worry, he says, this is nothing like that. **6**

So what's it like? A bit like the Space Probe at Wonderland. A bit like … look, to be honest, that plummeting-to-earth, falling-at-1,000-feet-every-5.5-seconds, chin-flapping-around-your-eyeballs, I-feel-sick-can-we-go-home-now type of feeling is not for me. **7**

But after 52 seconds free fall — that's right, count them, live them, breathe them, scream them, disbelieve them — the 'chute opens. And that floating-above-the-earth, human-turned-into-butterfly, dipping-this-way-and-that, toe-tingling, landscape-of-silence, leaf-floating-on-air-current, I'm-so-glad-I'm-still-alive type feeling is fantastic. **8**

PS: Arriving back at work, meet a colleague in the lift. 'What have you been up to lately?' she asks. Reply, 'Oh, I've just jumped out of a plane.' 'Where from?' she says. '13,000 feet,' I say. She's silent for a while. So are the others in the lift. Now I feel good. **9**

(*Sydney Morning Herald*, Spectrum, 17 January 1988, pp 1, 6)

UNDERSTANDING THE TEXT

Now read the text carefully. Answer the questions.

1 The writer does not explain everything to the reader. Instead she gives a hint and leaves the reader to infer (work out) the meaning. Answer these questions.

a How does Joanne feel about her jump (para 1)? Which word tells you this? ______________________

____

b Who is the one person left to jump (para 2)? How do you know? ______________________

c What does the writer mean when she says *to the womb maybe*? ______________________

____

d What are *speed limits, smoke-free zones, tight deadlines*, the *low-fat shopping* list, and the *SPF-15 routine* examples of? ______________________

e Why does the writer mention them here? ______________________

f What does the writer mean when she asks *Why Phil* (para 4)? ______________________

____

g Why does the writer say: *Wish he'd take the dark glasses off* (para 5)? ______________________

____

h Why is the writer worried by the fact that Craig has done almost 6,000 jumps (para 5)? __________

____

2 The writer uses hyphenated groups of words to convey the feeling of falling through the air (paragraphs 7 and 8). How does the writer convey the different speeds of the two stages of the skydive? (Hint: read the sentences out loud.)

____

____

3 On the basis of all that the writer says about her experience, which of the following do you think she would probably say to someone thinking about trying sky-diving.

a ______ Try it. It's terrific.

b ______ Don't try it. It's terrifying.

c ______ Only try it if you are insane.

d ______ Try it but be prepared to be sick with fear.

RESPONDING TO THE TEXT

1 The writer uses humour in many parts of the text. Underline any parts you found funny. How does the humour add to the effectiveness of the article? (Write or tell someone.)

2 Would you go for a skydive after reading this article? Why / why not? (Write or tell someone.)

SPOTLIGHT ON LANGUAGE

The writer uses many techniques to make the story interesting and amusing. How many of these did you notice? Can you find an example of each?

- Writing the story as if it is actually happening.
- Using very short sentences (e.g. *This is insane …*) .
- Using single words or small groups of words instead of sentences (e.g. *At 13,500 feet; looks*).

Tapioca to the rescue 20

Newspaper report
Understanding detail
Understanding main idea
Working out word meanings
Understanding newspaper language

PREPARING TO READ

answers page 138

Imagine you have a research task to make a poster about an environmental problem and possible solutions. Quickly skim this article to find out what it gives you *most* information about. (Circle one.)

a ______ the damage that plastic bags can do

b ______ solutions to the problem of plastic bags

c ______ facts and figures about plastic bag usage

Now read the text fully.

Tapioca to the Rescue

1 **A plastic bag dances gracefully in the film *American Beauty*. But the reality is bags are dangerous, clogging up drains, rivers and seas. Now a new brand of degradeable plastic may save the day, writes *Stephanie Peatling*.**

2 Plastic bags found some unlikely critics at the recent Bathurst 1000. As the cars zoomed around the track one of the favourites for the race, Ford team member Craig Lowndes, was forced out of competition after a plastic bag blew onto the track and clogged up his engine's air duct.

3 The eventual winner, Mark Skaife, thought he might not make it, too, after three plastic bags got into his engine. He dragged them around the track 20 times before finishing.

4 Long the scourge of environ-mentalists for their effect on wildlife, waterways and their inability to biodegrade, the plastic bag has come in for a pasting lately.

5 The environmental group Planet-Ark estimates Australians use six billion plastic bags a year, with more than half coming from supermarkets. It wants to see Australia go the way of Ireland which slugged a 15 Euro cent (about 25c) levy on every plastic bag dispensed by shops.

6 The Irish Government says the use of plastic bags has fallen by more than 90% since the levy was introduced in March. It has also raised 3.5 million euros for the Irish coffers which will be used for environmental projects. Britain has indicated it is considering a similar levy. But there is resistance within Australia to forcing retailers to change their ways. The Australian Retailers Association, which represents large retailers such as Woolworths, says a levy is a 'simplistic solution' which avoids addressing the real issue of 'inappropriate consumer behaviour'.

7 Stan Moore, the association's policy director, admits encouraging people to return their bags to the supermarket for reuse or recycling is not working. 'Consumers are well trained in household recycling and they do it for a variety of products. Why don't we add plastic bags and wrap and film to the existing recycling stream?'

8 The federal Environment Minister, David Kemp, has given the national Packaging Covenant Council six weeks to come up with specific proposals for actions to rid Australia of the plastic bag, including a response to a levy of some sort.

9 John Dee, the head of Planet Ark, says the days of the free plastic bag are over. 'It would be a critical mistake for the retail industry if they underestimated the public sentiment on this.'

10 Sixty BP stores are about to begin a trial with biodegradeable bags made from tapioca, and Dee has just placed an order for two million of the bags to give away to any similar curious retailer. Made in Malaysia, the tapioca bags are the cheapest biodegradeable variety available and almost comparable in price to the sorts of bags supermarkets use now.

11 Dee points to supermarket chain Aldi as having done the legwork for supermarkets. In NSW, the chain's 34 stores charge 15c for every plastic bag, resulting in customers reusing the bags they have brought. 'Aldi has proved that it can work in Australia and that it won't affect supermarkets,' Dee says.

12 'This is a chain that is favoured by the unemployed and pensioners, but if the Government is concerned it could start the introduction of a levy by supplying every household with three or four cloth bags.'

13 What to do about the plastic bag has been troubling governments all over the world for years. Germany, Denmark and Sweden have already imposed taxes on plastic bags. While Denmark managed to cut down its consumption of plastic bags by 70%, in Sweden time proved that consumers gradually adjusted to paying for bags and the tax did not cut down on use.

14 Earlier this year Bangladesh banned all polythene bags. They were blamed for the 1988 and 1998 floods that submerged two-thirds of the country after it was found discarded bags were choking the drainage system.

15 In South Africa, they have been dubbed the 'national flag' because so many can be seen flapping from fences and caught in bushes. But plans by the Government there to ban plastic bags were thwarted by retailers and the plastic industry.

16 Instead, plastic bags must now be a minimum thickness, with the aim of making it too expensive for retailers to give them away. Under the new regulations bags will have a minimum thickness of a thirtieth of a millimetre (less than one seven-hundredth of an inch), about double the average.

17 The hope is that South African consumers, who use an estimated 8 billion plastic bags a year, will change their behaviour and cut down if they are forced to pay, with retailers having to detail the cost of the bags so consumers can decide how many they want to pay for.

18 While retailers want the onus of responsibility to be on consumers, environmentalists say that choice needs to be made harder by making them pay for plastic bags.

19 As Dee says: 'Plastic bags are a bad habit we need to break.'

(*Sydney Morning Herald*, 25 October 2002, p. 14)

UNDERSTANDING THE TEXT

1 Who are these people?

a Craig Lowndes ______________________________

b Mark Skaife ______________________________

c Stan Moore ______________________________

d John Dee ______________________________

e David Kemp ______________________________

Which two are the *least* important to the article content? ______________________________

2 The groups below are mentioned in the article. Match each group to what they have done or want.

PlanetArk	Irish Government	Australian Retailers Association	Australian Government
BP stores	Aldi stores	Bangladesh Government	South African Government

a ____________________ charge 15 cents for bags

b ____________________ have banned bags

c ____________________ are trialling tapioca bags

d ____________________ made bags a minimum thickness

e ____________________ introduced a levy

f ____________________ wants a levy on plastic bags, will give two million tapioca bags to stores

g ____________________ asked for proposals for actions, including response to levy

h ____________________ does not want levy, wants plastic bags added to recycling system

3 True or false?

a John Dee believes the public doesn't want free plastic bags. True / False

b Plastic bag use in Ireland has fallen. True / False

c Plastic bag use in Sweden has fallen. True / False

d The South African action aims to make bags too expensive to be given away. True / False

4 Look back at your answer to the skimming question in Preparing to Read. What is your answer to the question now? Write a sentence to state the main idea of the article.

____

____

____

5 Journalists make frequent use of colloquial (conversational) language. Find these examples in the text. Then write down another way of expressing the same meaning.

a save the day (para 1) ____________________

b might not make it (para 3) ____________________

c come in for a pasting (para 4) ____________________

d go the way of (para 5) ____________________

e slugged (para 5) ____________________

f coffers (para 6) ____________________

g done the legwork (para 11) ____________________

h dubbed (para 15) ____________________

RESPONDING TO THE TEXT

Prepare a poster using key points from the article. If you wish you could look up other websites to gather more information (for example, Clean up Australia, Clean up the World, government departments for the environment, or community organizations, such as Greenpeace).

SPOTLIGHT ON LANGUAGE

'Tapioca to the rescue' is typical of many newspaper articles. Take notice of

- the short paragraphs
- the use of interesting and amusing information at the start
- the use of a headline which is not immediately comprehensible.

Why do newspaper journalists use these techniques?

Night of passage — Part One

Novel extract
Skimming to preview
Understanding main ideas
Inferring
Working out word meanings

PREPARING TO READ

answers page 138

Skim the text below for about 15 seconds and then circle one word to correctly complete each sentence.

a The text is about a boy / girl / woman / man.

b The text is set in the real world / in a fantasy world.

c The text is about a crime / a journey / a fight.

Check your answers after you have read the whole text.

NIGHT OF PASSAGE
by Lee Harding

Part One **paragraph**

When they came in sight of the city, Brin left the rest of the party behind and continued alone. **1**

The Elders settled down to wait. They prayed for her safe return, then drank wine and smoked ceremonial pipes and chanted the old songs. This also was part of the ritual, and they would keep it up without pause until she returned. **2**

Brin made good time across the open ground, her natural environment. Crouching low so her dark skin merged with the sunburned grass, she moved with a lithe step. Later, the going would not be so easy. **3**

The time was late afternoon and she planned to reach the outskirts of the city before dusk. She had no desire to enter this unknown labyrinth until daylight waned, and would bide her time until twilight, when the gathering darkness would afford her cover. **4**

When she considered the dangers that lay ahead of her, fear returned, but if she survived this long night of Passage tomorrow she would be a woman, and privy to the mysteries of her clan. Such was the nature of her trial. **5**

She paused to take stock of her surroundings. Choosing a suitable tree, she quickly scaled it and settled down high up among the sweet-scented branches to await the dusk. **6**

Nothing moved on the landscape. A swollen orange sun dipped slowly out of sight behind the ramparts of the distant city, the gaunt buildings silhouetted against the sunset like the escarpment of some forbidding mountain range. In the distance she imagined she could hear the ritual chanting of the Elders, wafted to her on the shoulders of the night-wind. She felt lonely and isolated, but she had no wish to turn back. Not when she had come so far. **7**

The world gradually darkened. When the first wan stars appeared overhead she clasped both hands together and whispered the Prayer of Passage, remembering home and family and brother Mark, who would make his run next summer. What tales they would share when he became a man! This done, she climbed down from her perch and set off at a brisk pace on the next stage of her journey. **8**

As she moved closer to the city, the fields became hazardous underfoot. They were littered with relics of the Old Ones and avoiding them made for slow progress. Brin angled towards the old road, confident this would lead her to the heart of the city, yet unwilling to betray herself by stepping onto it. Instead she followed the road at a discreet distance, crouching low so her fingers brushed the ground. Her senses ranged far ahead, alert for the slightest sound that would signal the presence of predators on this no-man's-land between the city and the open country. Occasionally the ruins of an ancient wheeled vehicle loomed before her and she gave these a wide berth. It was known that wild dogs and other dangerous animals used these hulks for shelter, and she had no desire to arouse their curiosity. **9**

Her right hand never strayed far from the knife sheathed at her waist and her left hand clutched the small bag of stones jostling against her thigh. Her body was covered with a rime of sweat, but she had no inkling of fatigue. She was no stranger to long treks, although this was the most hazardous she had undertaken. But despite her fears she drew courage from knowing that this night would conclude her quest for womanhood and provide a bridge between her childhood and the person she was destined to become. It was a long-established ritual of her people. **10**

(from *Dream Time*, Puffin Books, Melbourne, 1989, pp 45–7)

UNDERSTANDING THE TEXT

Read the whole text and then answer the following questions.

1 Read very carefully to find the *first* time the information below is given to the reader. The writer might not tell you this explicitly. (Write the paragraph number. You might use the same number twice or not use some numbers.)

______ Brin was travelling on her own.

______ Brin's journey was something she had to do to become a woman.

______ Brin is close to her family.

______ Brin would be in some danger on her journey.

______ Brin feels very alone.

______ Brin lived in a country area.

______ Brin wanted to complete the journey even though she was afraid.

______ Brin was not the first to do this journey.

2 Find the words in the text which have a meaning similar to the words and phrases below.

a slim and athletic (para 3) ______________________

b maze (para 4) ______________________

c floated (para 7) ______________________

d thin and angular (para 7) ______________________

e pale (para 8) ______________________

f appeared large (para 9) ______________________

g wisely judged (para 9) ______________________

h hint or sign (para 10) ______________________

i thin covering (para 10) ______________________

3 Find these parts of the text and think about the meaning of the phrases in *italics*. Write each one in different words.

a Brin *made good time* .... (para 3) ______________________

b Later, *the going would not be so easy*. (para 3) ______________________

c ... would *bide her time* until twilight. (para 4) ______________________

d ... when the gathering darkness *would afford her cover.* (para 4) ______________________

e ... and *privy to* the mysteries of her clan. (para 5) ______________________

f ... to *take stock of* her surroundings. (para 6) ______________________

g ... and avoiding them *made for* slow progress. (para 9) ______________________

h Her senses *ranged far ahead* ... (para 9) ______________________

i ... and she *gave these a wide berth*. (para 9) ______________________

j She was *no stranger to* long treks. (para 10) ______________________

4 The writer hints that a war or disaster of some kind has occurred in recent times. Write down all the evidence you can find which suggests this.

RESPONDING TO THE TEXT

Write a short description of Brin's physical appearance based on what you have read in this text and your imagination. If you prefer, draw a picture.

SPOTLIGHT ON LANGUAGE

The writer often uses poetic language. For example: *swollen orange sun; the gaunt buildings; silhouetted against the sunset; like the escarpment of some forbidding mountain range; on the shoulders of the night-wind.* Can you find other examples?

The writer uses some unusual words to create an image of the scene. Try to work out the general meaning of any words you did not know from the context. Then check the exact meanings in the dictionary. Add any new words to your personal dictionary if you have one (see suggestion on page 59).

Night of passage — Part Two 22

Novel extract
Predicting
Understanding detail
Inferring
Understanding complex sentences
Working out word meanings

PREPARING TO READ

answers page 139

Before you begin reading the next extract from *Night of Passage* (below), tick the two things you most expect it to tell you more about.

______ Brin's life with her family

______ the next stage of Brin's journey

______ Brin's clan

______ the city

______ the wild dogs

______ the countryside

Now read the text.

NIGHT OF PASSAGE

By Lee Harding

Part Two **paragraph**

Tonight the sky was clear and there would be a full moon to guide her. These were auspicious omens. The city would be a maze of darkness and the light of heaven her only ally; and when she arrived at the outskirts of the city several hours would remain before she reached the centre. This road would lead her there, to be sure, but for safety she would hug the shadows and side-streets and use the darkness to conceal her presence. If she made good time she hoped to reach her goal before midnight, then find somewhere safe to remain until morning. When dawn arrived she would select her trophy — this, too, was part of the ritual — and depart in haste before the daylight betrayed her. 1

She paused when she reached the outskirts of the city. The stark contours of the squat buildings were a jangling discord in her mind. They were so different from the homes of her people, which everywhere blended harmoniously with their surroundings. She felt a twinge of dread standing so close to strangeness but steeled herself to move closer, for she had need of the protective shadows. 2

In this devious way did she enter the abandoned city, a slender figure moving deeper into **3**
darkness, her senses alert for any sign of danger. Even now, so long after The Fall, it was known that the city was not entirely deserted. Strange stories had been told by previous initiates, although one could never be sure how much was fact and how much was mere fancy, intensified by fear and anxiety. But it was sobering to recall the youngsters who had failed to return from their night of Passage. Surely this was proof that the dangers still lurked in the city.

Much of what Brin knew about the city was either legend or hearsay, from which some **4**
useful facts could be gleaned. It seemed likely that wild dogs prowled the concrete canyons and it was assumed they would be more dangerous than their counterparts in the open country. Some experts insisted that animals of the plain would not dare venture inside the city, for fear of what they might find there. Brin was not prepared to take chances. She was determined to survive her night of Passage and attain her majority, although she wished for a companion to shore up her courage. It was customary for groups of two or three to make their run together, but this summer she was the only youngster to celebrate her 15th birthday and, as a consequence, was expected to make her run alone.

She hurried along crumbling footpaths, nimbly avoiding a variety of obstructions. The **5**
silence was strained and unnatural, unlike the silence of the open country, where small sounds were always present. But as her senses grew more attuned to these unfamiliar surroundings she realised that the silence was not as absolute as she had first thought. Far off, near the centre of the city, she heard faintly the sorrowful howl of some melancholy animal. Her scalp prickled with apprehension. She was too far from the source of the sound to be sure, but it reminded her of some disconsolate beast baying its loneliness to the night sky. She unsheathed her knife in preparedness as she moved deeper into the labyrinth.

(from *Dream Time*, Puffin Books, Melbourne, 1989, pp 47–8)

UNDERSTANDING THE TEXT

1 The words in italics refer to other things mentioned in the text. Find the full sentences and then read back to find what the words refer to.

a … her only *ally* (para 1). What would be her ally? ____________________

b … she hoped to reach *her goal* (para 1). What is her goal? ____________________

c … standing so close to *strangeness* (para 2). What is the strangeness? ____________________

d In this *devious way* … (para 3). Which devious *way*? ____________________

e … intensified by *fear and anxiety* (para 3). Whose fear and anxiety? ____________________

f … was not prepared to *take chances* (para 4). Take chances about what? ____________________

2 Answer these questions.

a Why does Brin need a *trophy* (para 1) and what does *trophy* mean in this context?

b What evidence is there in this text that Brin felt warmly towards her home?

c What does it mean that Brin *steeled herself* (para 2)?

d Is Brin likely to find people in the city? Give your reasons.

e In paragraph 3, what word is used to describe other young people who have gone through this ritual? What other words do you know that relate to this word?

f Why does Brin *not* believe all she has been told about the dangers?

g What two facts about the city does Brin feel pretty sure about?

h What do you think *attain her majority* might mean (para 4)? (Hint: Think about the purpose of Brin's trip. Also think about the meaning of *major* — most/biggest/most important.)

i How would a companion help Brin? ______

j As Brin gets closer to the centre, what sound does she hear, and how does it make her feel?

3 Read the sentences before and after the words below, and then decide if the word has a positive meaning (e.g. good, pleasant) or a negative meaning (e.g. bad, harmful). Write **P** or **N** for your answer. Then use your dictionary to write in a more exact meaning for the word as it is used in the text.

a auspicious (para 1) ______

b stark (para 2) ______

c squat (para 2) ____________________

d jangling (para 2) ____________________

e discord (para 2) ____________________

f harmoniously (para 2) ____________________

g lurked (para 3) ____________________

h melancholy (para 5) ____________________

i apprehension (para 5) ____________________

j disconsolate (para 5) ____________________

RESPONDING TO THE TEXT

1 Write a sentence to say what you think *The Fall* (para 3) might have been.

____

____

____

2 If Brin meets someone in the city, what do you imagine they would be like (e.g. appearance, speech, attitude to Brin)?

____

____

____

SPOTLIGHT ON LANGUAGE

The writer uses quite formal language to create a sense of a world of a different time and place. Look at these examples from both Parts One and Two, and write a sentence expressing the same meaning but in more informal everyday language. (Use your own paper.)

Part 1:

Such was the nature of her trial. (para 5)

What tales they would share when he became a man! (para 8)

Part 2:

... and depart in haste before the daylight betrayed her. (para 1)

In this devious way did she enter the abandoned city ... (para 3)

Rap music — the beginnings 23

Webpage
Skimming for preview
Understanding main ideas
Understanding complex sentences
Working out word meanings
Interpreting poetic language

PREPARING TO READ

answers page 139

1 Spend about 60 seconds thinking about what you know about rap music. Write down any words you know that relate to this kind of music. (Use your own paper.)

2 Skim the text below for 60 seconds, and tick off any words on your list that you saw in the text.

Now read the text carefully.

RAP MUSIC — THE BEGINNINGS

NEWS | REVIEWS | TOURS | ARTISTS

In the early 1970s a musical genre was born in the crime-ridden neighborhoods of the South Bronx. 1
Gifted teenagers with plenty of imagination but little cash began to forge a new style from spare parts. Hip-hop, as it was then known, was a product of pure streetwise ingenuity. Extracting rhythms and melodies from existing records and mixing them up with searing poetry chronicling life in the 'hood', hip-hop spilled out of the ghetto.

So writes Kurtis Blow, rap pioneer, who played a major role in launching the international 'rap attack' that revolutionised the music industry in the 1980s. He describes a quite astonishing period in 20th century cultural history, during which young teenagers, mainly African and Caribbean Americans, responded in an inspired and creative way to their neglected, poverty-stricken environment. They had no dance halls to dance in, so they danced in the streets. They had no musical instruments to play, so they used stereo equipment to make new sounds. They had no canvases to paint on, so they painted on walls and subway cars.

The terms 'hip-hop' and 'rap' are sometimes used interchangeably, but as Kurtis Blow explains it: 2

Rap is talking in rhyme to the rhythm of a beat. Hip-hop is a culture, a way of life for a society of people who identify, love and cherish rap, break-dancing, DJ-ing and graffiti.

The confusion between the two is not really surprising. In the first place, the original term for rap music *was* hip-hop. Also, at that time, the music was more about DJ mixing and re-mixing of records, than about talking in rhyme to rhythm, although these two ways of making music quickly merged.

The music of the hip-hop culture drew on many musical influences. At the time that rap emerged, 3
disco music was monopolising the airwaves. Many of the earliest hip-hop DJs used these disco sounds. Other DJs played rhythm and blues (R&B), soul, and funk. DJs played a vinyl record or two vinyl records at the same time. By manipulating the records as they played, they created new

songs with long instrumental segments (called breaks). In this way, the turntable became a musical instrument. A rapper (sometimes the DJ themself) would entertain the crowd during the instrumental breaks, making up their own words to accompany the music.

The new music immediately led to new ways of dancing, and break-dancing was born. Wherever the DJs played their new kind of music, the B-boys — beat boys, break boys or Bronx boys — danced. Only the best dancers would compete, showing off their best moves while a circle crowded around to watch. Watching the B-boys do 'battle' was usually the highlight of hip-hop nights at clubs and parties. Very quickly, break-dancing became a substitute for physical fighting for many youths and street gangs. **4**

After filling the streets, subways and clubs of the Bronx and then downtown New York with its unique sound, the music of the hip-hop culture migrated across the country to Los Angeles in the mid to late 80s, and developed its own distinctive musical style. The 80s also saw rap move from the fringes of hip-hop culture to mainstream music industry around the world, as white musicians began to embrace the style. Rap reached the top ten on the Billboard pop charts for the first time in 1986 with the Beastie Boys, and Run-DMC and Aerosmith. Not long after, a female rap group, Salt-N-Pepa made it into the top 20. In the later 1980s, strongly political rap was beginning to overtake the genre, and 'gangsta' rap with explicit references to sex, drugs and violence was also on the increase. Both these variants of the original rap music stirred up controversy and protest from parents, concerned about the language and attitudes their children were being exposed to. **5**

Today rap has become one of the most important musical forms of the 20th century. It draws on a wide range of musical influences but, perhaps more significantly, it has also become a major influence on other kinds of music. As Kurtis Blow remarks: **6**

Hip-hop is the voice of a generation that refused to be silenced by urban poverty, a local phenomenon fueled with so much passion and truth it could not help but reach the entire world.

(adapted from a number of different webpages)

UNDERSTANDING THE TEXT

1 Answer the questions.

a *Who* forged a new style of music? (para 1) ______

b *What* extracted rhythms and melodies from existing records? (para 1) ______

c What was *astonishing* about the period that Kurtis Blow describes. (para 1)

______

d The young people that Kurtis Blow describes did not only play music. What else did they do?

______

e Rap is the same as hip-hop. True or false? ______

f Name four kinds of music that influenced rap. ______

g *In this way,* the turntable became a musical instrument. In what way? (para 3) ________________

____

h What might the *B* in *B-boys* stand for? (para 4) ________________

i Many youths and gangs began to __________ instead of __________ (para 4)

j Rap music in Los Angeles was different from rap in New York. True or false?

k What does the writer suggest helped rap music move into the mainstream music industry?

____

l What kinds of rap music caused controversy and why?

____

____

m We can say that rap is now a major musical form because it draws on a wide variety of musical influences. True or false? ________________

2 Headings usually capture the main idea/s of text sections in a few words. Below are three possible headings for each of the six paragraphs in this text. For each paragraph, which heading best expresses the main idea/s? (Circle one.)

para 1:	Crime and poverty	Born in the ghetto	Kurtis Blow
para 2:	What the terms mean	DJ-ing and rap	Different kinds of rap
para 3:	Disco and rap	Influences and techniques	DJ techniques
para 4:	A new kind of dancing	Dancing not fighting	Other developments
para 5:	New York	Gangsta rap	Into the mainstream
para 6:	A major musical influence	Kurtis Blow's view	A passionate kind of music

3 Find words in the text that have a similar meaning to the words below.

a create (para 1) ________________

b brilliance (para 1) ________________

c telling (para l) ________________

d as if they mean the same (para 2) ________________

e love (para 2) ________________

f controlling (para 3) ________________

g edges (para 5) ________________

4 Kurtis Blow has a poetic way of writing. What does he mean by

a ... began to forge a new style *from spare parts*. (para 1)

b ... *searing* poetry (para 1)

c ... life in the *'hood* (para 1)

d ... *fueled with* so much passion (para 6)

RESPONDING TO THE TEXT

Write down your own personal opinion of rap music. Use the space below for your draft or notes, and then write your final copy on your own paper.

Human cloning

24

Letters to the editor
Understanding main ideas
Distinguishing between fact and opinion
Reading critically

PREPARING TO READ

answers page 140

1 Read this short explanation of cloning.

A clone is a genetic copy of an organism made from one original cell or individual (male or female). Humans have been cloning plants for years, but cloning animals had proved to be a lot more difficult. Then Dolly the sheep was cloned in 1996. Since then many other animals have been cloned. The idea of cloning humans is very controversial of course, but scientists say the technology is already here. There have now been a number of claims that human cloning has actually been done.

Are you *for* or *against* human cloning, based on what you know already? Give reasons.

____

____

UNDERSTANDING THE TEXT

Now read the letters to the editor opposite and answer the questions that follow.

1 Which of the letters to the editor are **for** cloning (**F**), **against** cloning (**A**) or **wanting debate** about cloning (**D**)?

Letter **1** ________ Letter **2** ________ Letter **3** ________ Letter **4** ________

Letter **5** ________ Letter **6** ________ Letter **7** ________ Letter **8** ________

2 Letters pages usually give a headline to each letter which expresses the main idea. Which letters do you think had the headlines below?

a Keep up research ______ **b** Accept the new ______

c Ban cloning now ______ **d** Just all wrong ______

e Need for rules ______ **f** Great opportunities ______

g Dangerous path ______ **h** Get serious ______

Letters To The Editor

Human Cloning

Reports of the first cloned human babies and the recent death of Dolly the sheep, the first cloned animal, have sparked another round of letters this week on the subject of human cloning.

Dolly, the sheep, showed the world that cloning mammals was possible. It is vital that research continues to demonstrate whether cloning is a cure or a curse for mankind. We can't stop now. But at the same time, let's talk about it, so that the moral and ethical dilemmas can be sorted out before we go too far. **1**

What's all the fuss? There is no good reason *not* to clone. Most arguments against it are based on wishy-washy feelings that it is in some way unnatural, or ridiculous fears that it will lead to another Hitler taking over the world with an army of identical super-beings. What rubbish! Cloning technology will open up tremendous opportunities for the sick and for those unfortunate people who cannot have children by normal means. Let's not allow stupid fears and anxieties to stop progress. **2**

It took a lot of time for the world to get used to the idea of a cloned animal, and despite Dolly's cute and appealing looks, we did not immediately accept her. We saw her as a freak. Now we are sad she is gone. But at the same time we are having trouble getting used to the idea that someone might have cloned a human being. In a couple of years we will have accepted that too. We treat new things with suspicion at first. But eventually we adjust. It's time we accepted cloning, and let the scientists get on with finding out its potential for the human race. **3**

Already parents are choosing the sex of their child. And already there have been made-to-order babies to solve serious family medical problems. In one recent case, a mother and father chose one embryo out of the many they produced through IVF treatment, to create a child with the matching bone marrow tissue needed to save their young son from leukaemia. While sympathetic to the families in these kinds of cases, I think we are going down a very dangerous path. It will not be long before parents are manipulating the birth process to get babies with blond hair, good sporting prowess or high intelligence. From there, governments might consider identifying individuals with the most useful genetic make-up and cloning them. Sound creepy? You betcha. **4**

The physical dangers of cloning have been well set out by scientists. There is evidence that clones may be prone to premature ageing. Clones are also likely to have more abnormalities than the non-cloned population. But the most serious dangers are ethical and moral. We must talk and act now to work out clear international rules about the uses of cloning. We do not want a world where cloning could be used to create a race of superhumans. **5**

There are probably some very good medical reasons to use cloning. I just can't think of one right now. But I can think of some very good reasons *not* to use cloning. First, it is unnatural. For example, it has the potential to upset the balance of males and females in the world. Second, it means we are 'playing God'. In the wrong hands, this power could be devastating for us all. And third, I'm sorry, but it simply feels wrong. And sometimes, I think, we should just listen to our gut feelings. **6**

Most arguments against cloning are weak. For example, people say it is unnatural, but nature creates clones all the time — as identical twins. They also say that cloning will be used for the wrong reasons — e.g. to create a child with movie-star looks or the musical talent of a Beethoven. But this is highly unlikely. Most parents would only consider cloning for extreme situations, for example, to replace a child who dies or to avoid a disease. We must not let these silly arguments dominate discussion. It is time to get serious, and examine how and when we might make use of cloning for the good of humankind. **7**

It may be good business to clone cows and sheep to get better agricultural products. However, we need to draw a line between human beings and the rest of the animal kingdom. We are not cows and sheep. The individuality of humans is something we must protect. Human cloning should be banned for all time, and banned now! **8**

3 It is important to distinguish between fact and opinion when reading Letters to the Editor.

a Read each letter again and decide if it is completely opinion (**O**), completely factual (**F**) or a mix of fact and opinion (**OF**). (Look back at Reading Critically, page 45, if needed.)

Letter **1** ________ Letter **2** ________ Letter **3** ________ Letter **4** ________

Letter **5** ________ Letter **6** ________ Letter **7** ________ Letter **8** ________

b Underline any facts you found.

4 **a** Letter 2 suggests that any reader who does not agree with the writer is stupid. Underline the words the writer uses to do this. Do you think this is a reasonable way to argue? Why / Why not?

____

____

b Which other letter makes the same suggestion, though less strongly? Underline the words in the letter that do this.

c Did Letter 2 make you move *towards* the writer's view, move *away* from the writer's view, or a little of both? Explain your answer.

____

____

d Which letter (or letters) did you find the most convincing, based on their use of fact or on the way they expressed their opinion? Explain your answer.

____

____

RESPONDING TO THE TEXT

Read back over the letters and underline any points you found especially interesting. Write a short paragraph now giving your views on human cloning. (Use your own paper.)

SPOTLIGHT ON LANGUAGE

When writing to persuade, writers use language which suggests that the reader and writer are part of the one group, already seeing the issue in the same way. For example, they use *we* or *let's* instead of *I;* as in Letter 5 — *We do not want a world …*; or in Letter 1 — *… let's talk about it …*

We must look out for these techniques, and think carefully about whether or not we *do* see the issue the same way as the writer.

Games — Part One

Novel extract
Predicting
Inferring
Understanding main ideas
Working out word meanings
Understanding detail

PREPARING TO READ

answers page 140

1 The cover of the book *Games* depicts a teenage girl reaching out towards a large glass object. It looks like she is trying to stop the glass shattering, but it is clearly too late. The look on the girl's face is of absolute terror. The room behind her is dark and gloomy. The letters of the book-title 'Games' are broken up into pieces and the words *Just a game ... but who — or what — is playing?* appear next to the girl's head.

The text on the next page is from the first page of *Games*. Read the text up to ... *is really pretty* (para 4). Which of the three girls is likely to be the girl on the cover? Give your reasons.

____

____

2 The initial dialogue quickly introduces the reader to the story. What do you find out about the setting, the situation and the characters from this dialogue?

____

____

UNDERSTANDING THE TEXT

1 Now read up to ... *a piano* (end of paragraph 5). Answer true or false based on what you have read so far.

a Patricia has been invited on the trip by Genevieve. True / False

b Kirsty is unhappy about Patricia being with them. True / False

c Genevieve is unhappy about Patricia being with them. True / False

d Patricia thinks that both girls want her with them. True / False

e Patricia is aware that her talking is not a good idea in the situation. True / False

Now read the whole text and answer the following questions.

GAMES

By Robin Klein

Part One

paragraph

'It's not all that far now, just uphill for a bit, then this path should join the gravel road leading up to the house,' Kirsty promised. 'We'll be there in no time.' **1**

'Which is exactly what you claimed one hour ago,' Genevieve said distantly. 'You said it was only a half-hour walk from the station.' **2**

'Well, I haven't been here for about six months, have I? It's not my fault, all this getting lost. Things get a bit muddled when you haven't been back to places for a long time.' **3**

'I don't mind the walk,' Patricia Miggs said eagerly. 'This track is really pretty.' **4**

They both glanced at her briefly, with not exactly contempt, but something so akin that she curled up inside, as embarrassed as a captain running his ship aground. It had been quite obvious from the moment they'd met, as arranged, at the main city railway station, that Kirsty Meadows regretted inviting her, and Genevieve Tait was angry about the invitation having been issued at all. Not letting well enough alone, she heard herself babbling on, filling the silence with tinkling words like insubstantial notes played at random on a piano. **5**

'Gosh, look at those ferns! They're just like tiny little green hands reaching out, aren't they? And the wattle coming out so early...ooh, you're so *lucky*, Kirsty, having an aunt who lives in the bush! I wish I had a little cottage up here, too.' **6**

'It's not a cottage.' **7**

'What?' **8**

'My Aunt Maude's place. It's not a cottage. I already told you that, Patricia, only you obviously didn't bother to listen properly. It's a big house.' **9**

'It's going to have to be big if we're to find it in all this jungle,' Genevieve said and moved away with her back registering bad-tempered disapproval. **10**

Patricia felt quite inadequate as she gazed after that straight back. Genevieve — long silky hair the colour of milk coffee, skin as pale as yoghurt, rain-coloured eyes that gave nothing away, but looked at you like the screen of a computer waiting for input. But unlike a computer, she gave nothing back. **11**

'I don't know what Genevieve's being so snaky for,' Kirsty muttered crossly. 'She didn't even get scratched in those blackberries like I did, and I'm not making a big deal about it. Honest, if she's going to spend the whole weekend bellyaching ...' **12**

Thrilled to be included in an unexpected confidence, Patricia whispered back, 'Yes, she's inclined to carry on a bit sometimes, isn't she? Maybe she'll be nicer when we get to your Aunt's house. It's just because it's so perishing cold out here. You know how Genevieve hates waiting around at the tram stop, too, in winter ...' **13**

But Kirsty, not particularly interested in what she had to say, had hurried on to catch up with Genevieve, appeasement in her voice. 'Gen, hang on a bit! Look, I told you so! There's the road, or at least it's supposed to be one, and there's Aunty Maude's place, spot on. So you can quit acting so toffee-nosed now.' **14**

(Puffin Books, Melbourne, 1986, pp 1–3)

2 **a** Where are the three girls going? ______________________________

b When Kirsty tell the girls the house is big, how does Genevieve show she is still unhappy with the situation?

____

c Why does Patricia feel inadequate when she looks at Genevieve?

____

d In what way is Genevieve like a computer?

____

e In what way is she not like a computer?

____

f Patricia is happy when Kirsty is cross with Genevieve. Why?

____

g After reading the last paragraph, how would you compare the way Kirsty feels about Patricia and the way she feels about Genevieve.

____

3 Find words in the text that mean the same as these words.

a hate, disregard (para 5) ______________

b similar to (para 5) ______________

c making things worse not better (para 5) ______________

d not good enough (para 11) ______________

e complaining (para 12) ______________

f snobbish (para 14) ______________

g peace, making up (para 14) ______________

4 Do you think that the writer's overall purpose in this text is to show the reader: (circle one)

a the physical setting (location, landscape).

b the reason the girls are on a trip together.

c the relationships between the three girls.

d the relationship between Patricia and Kirsty.

RESPONDING TO THE TEXT

Think again about the question in the Preparing to read section. Do you still have the same opinion about the girl on the cover? Why or why not?

____

Games — Part Two

Novel extract
Skimming
Understanding main ideas
Understanding detail
Working out word meanings

PREPARING TO READ

answers page 140

Keeping in mind what you have read in Part One of *Games*, skim Part Two for 15 seconds. The text mainly consists of (tick one):

a ______further conversation between the girls.

b ______a description of the house.

c ______Patricia's thoughts about the other girls.

d ______Patricia's fears about the house.

GAMES

By Robin Klein

Part Two

paragraph

Patricia trailed after them, carrying, besides a bunch of wildflowers she'd picked along the way, her own gear, Kirsty's heavy cassette radio, a plastic bag of tapes and most of the food. Being laden with all those extra things was her own fault. She'd offered to carry them, even though the load was really far too heavy for someone of her slight physique. Kirsty and Genevieve strode on unencumbered by little more than their overnight bags, not even glancing back to make sure she was coping. Clutching all the parcels in her aching arms, she made one last effort and caught up. She stared up at the old house, slumbering in a hammock of foliage. It seemed to have germinated there like some hybrid flower, to lie suspended amongst branches of tightly interwoven shrubs and bushes. 1

One often saw similar houses, especially on the outskirts of any city, all built to the same pattern: front door placed in the centre of a façade, steeply pitched galvanized roof, veranda hugging the façade to combat a climate that held exaggerated extremes of weather. Aunt Maude's house was distinguished by having an upper storey, also with a veranda of decorative cast iron, and if it had been in a different setting, a broad, flat site perhaps, it would have been just as charming as any other old colonial house. 2

But against the steep incline of the slope, it was as though an alien structure had slid down the hill at some stage and come dourly to rest. It seemed choked in its lush vegetation, its proportions faulty against the dominating bulge of land at its back. Its windows, three on either side of the front door and a long expanse on the upper level, were hooded by the verandas and gave the house a secretive air, like a suspicious face peering out from under a brimmed hat. 3

4 'Wow! I never realised it was this big!' Patricia said, awed, in spite of the house's unfriendly appearance. 'Your aunt must be ...' She was going to say 'rich', but thought better of it because it sounded crass. 'Your aunt must find it hard looking after such a huge place on her own.'

5 'She has someone in every now and then to clear the garden,' Kirsty said indifferently. 'Probably someone just as decrepit as she is, by the look of those weeds. Gawd, talk about Dracula's Castle!'

6 From the driveway, neglect and dilapidation were more noticeable; paint vanished completely from window frames, slatted shutters thick with damp cobwebs, thistles and dandelions starring the unmown lawn. The front door had a stained-glass panel, but one of the glass inserts was missing and had been replaced by plywood. A wooden tub on either side of the door held stringy miniature cypress trees, embedded in layers of old cigarette butts and stray rubbish.

7 'Aunt Maude always leaves a spare key under the third flowerpot on the left,' Kirsty said. Original, huh?'

8 'I read an article where it said it's just not safe to do that. Burglars can find any key in ten minutes at the very most, no matter where it's been hidden. What your aunt should do ...'

9 'All right, we get the picture,' Kirsty said impatiently, and Patricia shut up. Kirsty tilted the third flowerpot and pulled out a heavy, old-fashioned key. She unlocked the stained-glass door, which swayed briefly on its hinges and balked halfway, grudgingly questioning their right of entrance. Genevieve pushed the door wide open and strode inside as though she owned the house.

(Puffin Books, Melbourne, 1986, pp 3–5)

UNDERSTANDING THE TEXT

Now read the text carefully and then complete the following questions.

1 Answer true or false.

- **a** Kirsty and Genevieve had forced Patricia to carry most of the load. True / False
- **b** Patricia had picked some wildflowers. True / False
- **c** Patricia was not a large person. True / False
- **d** Kirsty and Genevieve carried their overnight bags and nothing else. True / False
- **e** Kirsty and Genevieve did not show any concern about Patricia's load. True / False
- **f** The house was totally surrounded and covered by plants of various kinds. True / False
- **g** The basic structure of the house was unusual. True / False
- **h** The house was not charming or attractive. True / False
- **i** The house was well taken care of. True / False

2 Find these words in the text and then underline the word beside it that best matches the meaning.

a	**unencumbered** (para 1)	not loaded up	loaded up
b	**hammock** (para 1)	a kind of hanging bed	a kind of garden
c	**foliage** (para 1)	plant leaves	hillside
d	**germinated** (para 1)	grown from seed	decayed
e	**façade** (para 2)	veranda	front of a building
f	**distinguished** (para 2)	spoilt	made different
g	**dourly** (para 3)	happily	unhappily
h	**crass** (para 4)	rude, offensive	stupid, ignorant
i	**indifferently** (para 5)	without interest	with interest
j	**decrepit** (para 5)	useless	broken down and old
k	**dilapidation** (para 6)	ugliness	ruin and decay

3 The writer describes the house and its setting in detail. Which of the following drawings best matches the description.

a

b

c

RESPONDING TO THE TEXT

1 Think back to question **1** in Preparing to read, in Part One (p. 101). Have you changed your mind about who is the girl on the book cover? If so, Why?

____

2 Based on your reading of Part One and Two of the extract from *Games* and the description of the book's cover, write down your ideas on the following questions. Why did Kirsty invite Genevieve and Patricia to her aunt's house, especially when she does not seem to like Patricia? What kind of things happen when they are inside the house?

____

____

____

____

____

____

____

____

____

____

____

____

____

____

SPOTLIGHT ON LANGUAGE

The writer uses metaphor and simile to describe the house. These give the impression that the house is alive and even has a will of its own. Following is one example. Can you find others?

... slumbering in a hammock of foliage. It seemed to have germinated there like some hybrid flower, to lie suspended amongst branches of tightly interwoven shrubs and bushes. (para 1)

27

Youth smoking drops and mobiles get credit

Newspaper report

Predicting • Understanding graphs
Understanding main ideas • Reading critically
Distinguishing fact and opinion

PREPARING TO READ

answers page 141

1 Read the headline and sub-headline of the article below and then look at the graph on the next page. What do you think the article will tell you? (Circle one.)

- **a** Youths are smoking less / more.
- **b** Youths are using mobile phones less / more.
- **c** Smoking and mobile phone use may be related / is probably not related.

Now read the article in full.

Youth Smoking Drops And Mobiles Get Credit

Teenage smoking has declined in Australia for the first time in a decade, writes Mark Ragg.

1 British anti-smoking activists, noting a similar decline there, argue that the cause may be the popularity of mobile phones, which offer young people adult style and street credibility.

2 The NSW Health Department confirmed the trend yesterday.

3 'There appears to be a slight decline in the rate of 12 to 17 year olds who reported smoking in the last week,' a spokeswoman said, while noting that the figures had yet to be collated and confirmed.

4 Smoking by Australian teenagers declined gradually from the 1960s but then rose fairly markedly in the 1990s.

5 In a letter today in the *British Medical Journal*, now the BMJ, the director of Action on Smoking and Health (UK), Mr Clive Bates, argues that mobile phones may be responsible for the recent decline.

6 British figures show the proportion of 15 year olds smoking dropped from 30% in 1996 to 25% last year.

7 At the same time, mobile phone use rose dramatically, with 70% of 17 year olds owning one.

8 Mr Bates said teenagers smoke, in part, because cigarettes offer them adult style, individuality, sociability, rebellion, peer-group bonding and adult aspiration.

9 Focus group research shows that mobile phones do much the same thing, with 12 to 15 yearolds saying they offered street cred.

10 'Mobile phones provide teenagers with something to do with their hands, give confidence, comfort, relief of boredom, and fulfil social and fun needs in much the same way that smoking does,' Mr Bates said.

11 Mobiles are also expensive, so teenagers faced with a choice between an 'old technology' (cigarettes), and a new technology (phone with text messaging, email and games) may dump the smokes, he said.

12 Australian anti-smoking experts contacted were interested in the theory, but non-committal.

13 They believe the Federally funded 'every breath you take' campaign started in 1996, may have had an impact, even though it targeted adults.

14 'Still, it's worth a look,' said one.

(*Sydney Morning Herald*, 4 November 2000, p. 2)

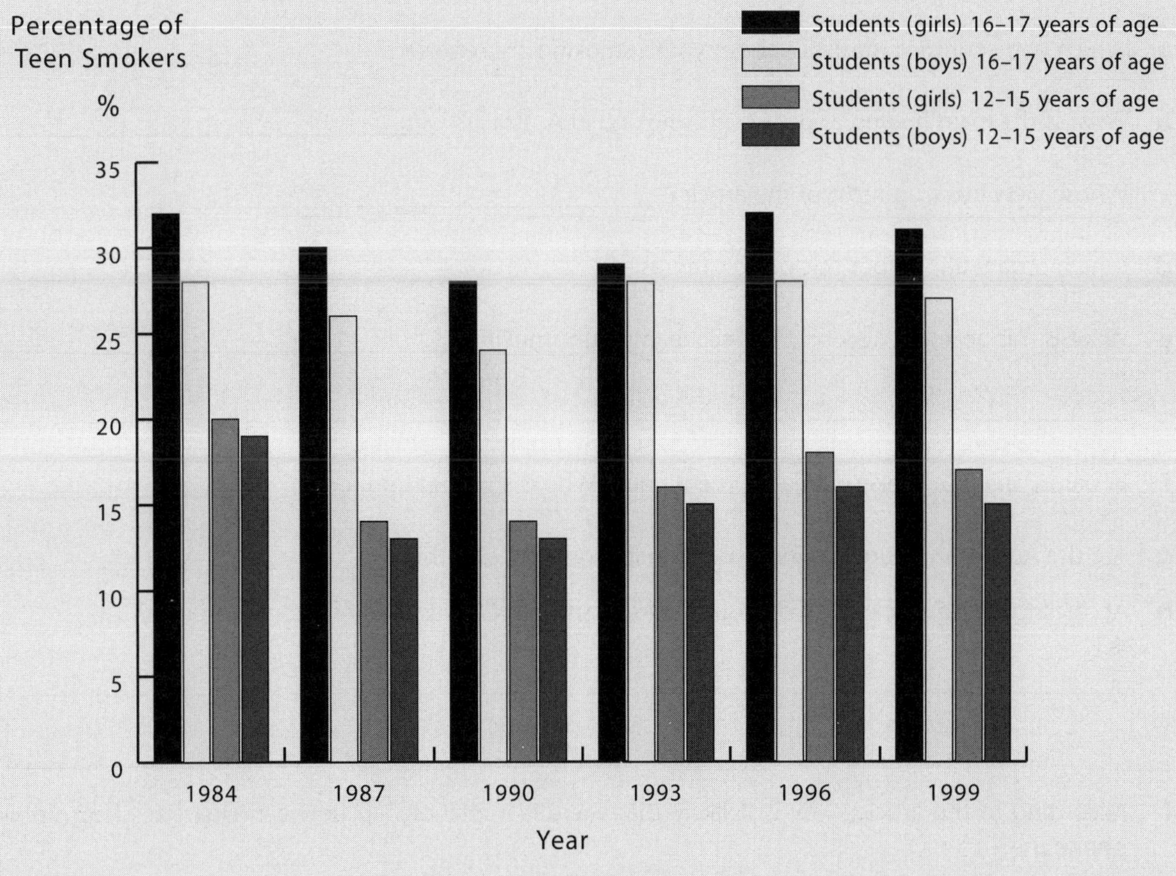

Source: Australian and New Zealand Journal of Public Health 1999, Vol. 23, No. 3

UNDERSTANDING THE TEXT

1 Look again at the graph *only*. Which statements below are true and which are false?

a	16–17 year olds smoke more than 12–15 year olds.	True / False
b	Boys of all ages smoke more than girls.	True / False
c	Boys aged 12–15 smoke more than girls.	True / False
d	The lowest rate for 12–15 year olds was from 1987 to 1990.	True / False
e	Smoking by both groups has been declining since 1996.	True / False
f	In 1999, about 16–17% of boys aged 12–15 smoked.	True / False
g	In 1996, about 23% of boys aged 16–17 smoked.	True / False
h	The difference between boys and girls rates is greater for the older age group.	True / False

2 Answer these questions about the text.

a Which two countries' statistics about youth smoking are reported? ______

b What is the main finding about youth smoking in Australia? ______

c Whose view takes up most of the article? ______

d Which organisation does this person represent? ______

e What is this person's view on the decline in youth smoking? ______

______

f In paragraph 3, a spokeswoman is mentioned. Who is she speaking for? ______

g Are the Australian figures definite yet? Which words tell you this? ______

h According to the article, why do young people smoke? Give as many reasons as you can.

______

______

i According to the article, why is it likely that there is a relationship between cigarettes and mobile phone use?

______

______

j According to the article, why is it likely that young people may choose *either* to use mobile phones *or* to smoke cigarettes, instead of doing both?

______

______

3 The article is a mix of fact and opinion about youth smoking. Thinking about the text *only* (*not* the graph), what percentage, roughly speaking, would you say is fact? (Circle one.)

10% 25% 50% 75% 90%

4 The article says that Australian anti-smoking experts are interested, but *non-committal* about the mobile phone theory — that is, they are not saying they believe it. Why do you think this is?

Think about these questions: Is the theory proven by research yet? Is it from Australia or overseas? What campaign do these experts say could be causing the decline? Why might they prefer this campaign to be the cause? NOTE: You can't be sure that any of these issues are the reason. But you should be thinking about these kinds of things if you want to be a critical reader.

RESPONDING TO THE TEXT

1 What do you think of the theory presented in the article? Write one or two paragraphs giving your reasons. If you wish you could write it as a Letter to the Editor. Use the space below for your draft or notes, and then write your final copy on your own paper.

2 Do a web search for more information about youth smoking.

Social comment

28

Cartoons
Understanding visual texts
Inferring
Reading critically

PREPARING TO READ

answers page 141

1 Cartoons like those opposite are called **social comment cartoons**. Give the cartoons one quick glance *only*, and write down what you think the cartoonist is commenting on.

Cartoon 1 ______________________________

Cartoon 2 ______________________________

2 If you saw these cartoons in the newspaper, would you stop to read them? Why / why not?

____

UNDERSTANDING THE TEXT

Now look closely at the cartoons and answer the questions.

1 Tick the comments below that you think the cartoonist is making in Cartoon 1. (You can choose more than one.) Then circle what you think is the main comment.

a ______ People shouldn't take mobile phones on bushwalks.

b ______ Using new technology can become a substitute for experiencing the real world.

c ______ Text messaging takes far too long to do.

d ______ People these days want to be in contact with others all the time.

e ______ People are allowing technology to take over their lives.

f ______ Men don't know how to communicate with women these days.

2 Now do the same for Cartoon 2.

a ______ Vending machines are increasing.

b ______ Gun use is increasing.

c ______ The world is more and more accepting of violence.

d ______ Young people are getting more violent.

e ______ Adults are feeling upset by some changes in their world.

f ______ It is easy to buy guns in our society.

Cartoon 1

Cartoon 2

3 **a** Cartoonists have to convey their meaning in a few simple pictures. In Cartoon 1, what does the changing scenery in the first four pictures tell us?

____

b In Cartoon 1, four pictures are used to show the young man sending the text message. One picture is used to show his girlfriend receiving it. What does this difference say about text messaging?

____

c In Cartoon 1, the last picture shows a city cafe scene. Why do you think the cartoonist decided to have the girlfriend receive the message there?

____

4 Cartoonists use simple pen strokes to convey a lot of meaning.

a In Cartoon 1, the young man's eyes are looking downwards and his mouth is fixed in a grin. What does this tell us?

____

b In Cartoon 2, how does the cartoonist convey with simple pen strokes that, in the scene, getting a gun from a vending machine is seen as a normal everyday activity? (Hint: Look at the boy's stance in the third picture, and the man's stance in all four pictures.)

____

____

5 Every word in a cartoon carries important meaning. Meaning is also conveyed by an absence of words.

a In Cartoon 1, how else could the cartoonist have conveyed that the young man is sending a text message?

____

b Do you think this would have been more or less effective than the 'tap tap'? ______________

6 **a** In Cartoon 2, what does the first speech bubble make you think about the subject of the cartoon?

____

b Does the second speech bubble keep up this impression or change it? ______________

c The third speech bubble has no speech bubble. What effect does this have?_

____

d The words in the last speech bubble show what the cartoon is really about. They also add to the idea that getting a gun from a vending machine is seen as a normal everyday activity. How do they do this?

____

____

7 Cartoonists often draw characters with exaggerated features. This sometimes leads to stereotypical images* of different social groups — sometimes harmful or insulting to these groups, and sometimes not. Are there any stereotypes in these cartoons? If so, are they harmful or insulting in any way to the groups they represent?

____

____

*A **stereotypical image** or a **stereotype** is a fixed set of characteristics for a particular type of person or thing — characteristics which are wrongly believed to be shared by all these people or things.

8 Go back to questions **1** and **2** about the possible comment the cartoonist is making. Have you changed your mind at all after doing activities 3–7? Change your answers now if you have.

RESPONDING TO THE TEXT

1 Write your own comment on an issue raised by either of the cartoons. Use the space below for your draft or notes, and then write your final copy on your own paper.

____

____

____

____

____

____

____

____

____

____

____

____

____

____

2 Over the next few weeks, have a look through some newspapers and magazines to find more cartoons like this. You will probably not understand them all — especially ones about politics, but it is good to get practice in reading these kinds of visual texts now.

The Gathering

Novel extract

Predicting • Understanding detail • Understanding cultural references
Inferring • Working out word meanings • Understanding complex sentence

PREPARING TO READ

answers page 142

1 Read the first paragraph *only* of the text below. What kind of book do you think *The Gathering* might be? (Circle one.)

science fiction fantasy social realism horror comedy the supernatural

2 What do you think *premonition* means? Think about the prefix *pre* in other words you know (e.g. *preview, predict, prelude*).

___

Read the text carefully and answer the questions.

THE GATHERING

paragraph

By Isabelle Carmody

Sometimes you get a feeling about a thing that you can't explain; a premonition of wrongness. Mostly you ignore it the way you would a little kid tugging at your sleeve. You think: what do kids know anyhow? **1**

We drove into the outskirts of Cheshunt at the tail end of an early autumn day, cold and crisp and fading to gold. Sunshine slanting though the car window rested in my lap, warm and heavy as a cat. **2**

I was sleepy and a bit woozy from reading my way through a stack of Phantom comics. As a rule I am not the kind of guy who goes in for stories about superheroes from Krypton or talking ducks and dogs. I like National Geographic, but I was reading these comics because the solicitor had sent them in a box along with a lot of my father's things that had not sold at auction. **3**

My mother thought comics were rubbishy. She had only read factual books and medical journals. I had just been a little kid when my parents were divorced, and they had not kept in contact but I always had a clear picture of him in my mind as a big serious man. The comics were a surprise and made me wonder what there was about him that I did not know. Naturally I had tried asking my mother but as usual she said she couldn't remember what he used to read, and that it was A Long Time Ago. She drives me crazy the way she acts so secretive about him, especially now. **4**

Suddenly she coughed in the dry fussy way she has of getting my attention before she says something. I waited for her to go on again with her usual speech of us making a new start, but she just nodded sideways. **5**

'That's your new school, Nathaniel.' **6**

Your school, I thought, because she chose it, just like she chose all the others. Her face had a closed look and she was staring straight ahead, concentrating on the road. **7**

So I looked. **8**

The school was a square, slab-grey complex set on an asphalt island in the middle of a common, running away to dry, bare-looking flatlands. She had told me Cheshunt was close to the sea. 'You can go to the beach on weekends,' she had said, as if it were across the road from our new house. Except there was no sign of the sea and the skyline bristled with pipes belching smoke into the sky. **9**

Closer to the school, I noticed there were no trees or shrubs around the buildings. In fact, Three North looked a lot like a concentration camp. The few bushes along the roadside were stunted and shriveled, with empty branches on the side that bore the brunt of the gritty wind flowing across the low hills and over the school. Cold air blew through the window, a bitter blast straight from the arctic. **10**

I lifted my hand to close the window, but it was shut. I looked around but all of the windows were wound up. Even the vents were closed. There was no way that wind could get into the car, yet I could see the fine downy hairs on my arm flatten under its force. **11**

I looked at my mother, who wore only a light, sleeveless shirt. She did not notice the wind, though her hair was whipping into her face and eyes. **12**

Fear crept through skin and bone and folded itself in my chest as I looked back at the school and felt that wind; the same kind of shapeless terror I felt when she took me to look at my father in his coffin before they closed it and put him in the ground. **13**

'You don't have to,' she said nervously, after doing a song and dance to get me there. It bothered her that I asked so many questions about him. Her wanting me to see the body was so bizarre that I guessed she had this stupid idea that I would forget about him once I saw that he was really dead and gone. But when it came to it, she seemed jittery and uneasy. Maybe she was a bit scared herself, of what we would see. I went forward, drawn by dread and morbid curiosity. **14**

He had been much thinner than I remembered. It seemed as if death had shrunken him, sucked the bigness out of him. His hair has gone straight and his limbs were stiff as a dried-flower arrangement. **15**

'He's so small,' my mother had said in a shocked whisper, as if he was sick instead of dead; as if loud voices would disturb him. **16**

Looking down at that strange, still face, I had barely been able to control the watery horror in my gut. I was suddenly terrified of being so close to a dead body; terrified that by staying there I might somehow catch death. **17**

That's how I felt, staring out of the car window at Three North; like I was looking at something wrong and unnatural; something dead; something bad that might be catching. Might get up and come after me. **18**

And the old nightmare seemed to hover about me, almost real, one stage from visible; the nightmare of running through a dark, wild forest with a monster after me. A shambling, leering thing with a shark's smile, whose reeking breath filled the air around me; the monster that was, since the funeral, sometimes my father, and above, a bloody, full moon riding high in the black night. **19**

But I just sat, still as a bone, tongue glued to the roof of my mouth, eyes watering from the force of the wind. **20**

The car glided around the corner and I let the memory of what had happened slip through the fingers of my mind like fine sand. **21**

Because a feeling like that has no more business being in my life than a dead father. **22**

(Puffin Books, Melbourne, 1993, pp xi–xiii)

UNDERSTANDING THE TEXT

1 **a** What is the name of the school? ______________________________

b What is the name of the town? ____________________

c Why was Nathaniel reading comic books in the car? ____________________

d Why was Nathaniel surprised to find that his father read comic books? ____________________

e Why is it strange that Nathaniel can feel the wind? ____________________

f What experience in his past does the wind make Nathaniel think about? ____________________

g What was the same about Nathaniel's feeling during both this past experience and the present one at the school? ____________________

h Nathaniel describes a nightmare he has often had. How did the nightmare change after his father's death? ____________________

2 Which of these drawings best matches the description of the school?

a

b

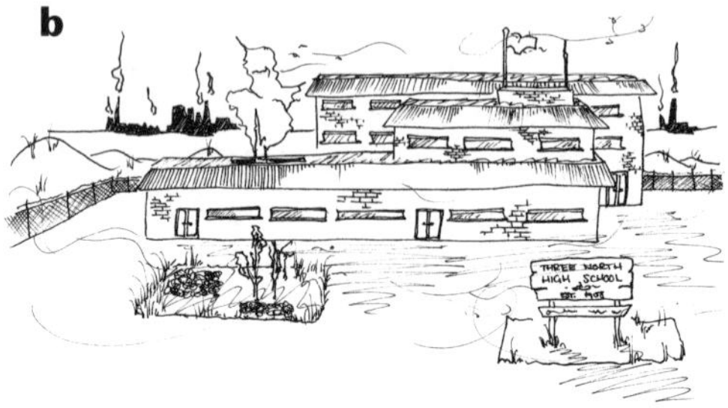

c

3 Writers often refer to certain social and cultural events or experiences, and assume their readers will understand them. What is the writer referring to when she mentions the following?

a superheroes from Krypton ____________________

b talking ducks and dogs ____________________

c National Geographic ____________________

4 Writers often tell us about the plot and characters in indirect ways. We, as readers, have to **infer** what is meant. What can you infer from the following information? (NOTE: Don't just write what the sentence means.)

a Nathaniel likes reading National Geographic. (para 3) ____________________

b Nathaniel's father's possessions were sold at auction. (para 3) ____________________

c His mother only reads factual books and medical journals. (para 4)

____

d Nathaniel was surprised that his father read comic books. (para 4)

___

e Nathaniel expects his mother to give her usual speech about making a new start. (para 5)

___

f Nathaniel's mother had a closed look when she mentioned the new school. (para 7)

___

g Nathaniel noticed the wind but his mother did not. (para 11/12)

___

h Nathaniel let the memory of what had happened slip out of his mind. (para 20)

___

5 Look through the text and find all the mentions Nathaniel makes about his mother. Based on these, what do you think is his attitude towards his mother?

___

6 Find these words in the text and use the context to work out their meanings. Write one other word you could use for each. Then check the meanings in your dictionary. (Note: Don't worry if you have not got it exactly right. This is not always possible to do from context. It is important, however, to try to do this.)

a common (para 9) ___

b belching (para 9) ___

c stunted (para 10) ___

d bore the brunt of (para 10) ___

e jittery (para 14) ___

f morbid (para 14) ___

g leering (para 19) ___

h reeking (para 14) ___

RESPONDING TO THE TEXT

1 The writer refers to feelings, events and experiences that occur in many young people's lives today. Look back through the story and make a list of these, and then say why you think the writer does this. (Use your own paper.)

2 Look back at question **1** in Preparing to read. Would you change your prediction now? If so, how?

3 How interested are you in reading the rest of this book? Give your reasons. Use your own paper.

SPOTLIGHT ON LANGUAGE

The story is told in the first person (*I, we*) by the main character. Look back over the text and think about how the story would be different if the writer had referred to the main character throughout in the third person *(he)*.

What effect does the use of the first person have on you as a reader — e.g. your interest in the character and his experiences?

The Lord of the Rings: The Two Towers

30

Film review
Understanding main ideas
Inferring
Understanding writer's purpose
Understanding detail
Working out word meanings

PREPARING TO READ

answers page 143

1 Have you seen *The Lord of the Rings: The Two Towers*? If so, did you like it? ____________________

2 Jot down 5 words you would use to describe the film, based on what you have heard about it or based on your own viewing.

____

3 What do you think is the purpose of film reviews in newspapers? Number these purposes **1–3** in order of importance.

______ To entertain

______ To persuade

______ To inform

Now skim the review on the following page for about 60 seconds to get a general idea of the content. Then read the review in full.

The Lord of The Rings: The Two Towers

Cast: Elijah Wood, Sean Astin, Ian McKellen, Viggo Mortensen, Christopher Lee, Mirando Otto, Orlando Bloom, John Rhys-Davies, Cate Blanchett, Andy Serkis
Director: Peter Jackson

1 To be honest I did not expect to be at all interested in *The Lord of the Rings* trilogy. But then I saw the first film, *The Fellowship of the Ring,* and I was hooked. Totally.

2 For years I have bored my friends rigid about violence in movies and special effects taking over from good storylines, and the trend towards superheroes and heroines rather than rich, complex, true to life characters.

3 But there I was going to see *The Fellowship* more than once (four times to be exact), then being the first on the block to buy the DVD, and even watching every single one of the DVD Special Features, which I usually find a complete yawn.

4 Anyway, as you can imagine, I was keenly awaiting the second film in the trilogy, *The Two Towers*. And I was not disappointed. Director Peter Jackson's achievement in bringing J.R.R. Tolkien's epic tale to the screen is truly remarkable. Jackson had a vision, and he persevered against some extraordinary odds to make his vision reality — not least of which was making three movies at the same time!

5 So, to the film itself. The plotline of Tolkien's book is, to say the least, difficult to summarise, and you can't really start in the middle, so first, a quick recap of the first film for those few souls who might not have seen it.

6 *The Fellowship of the Rings* told the story of Frodo Baggins (Wood), a hobbit, who has been given the task to destroy a magical ring, which, in the wrong hands (and there are many of these), would unleash unimaginable evil and destruction upon Middle Earth.

7 Middle Earth is the world which the hobbits inhabit, along with a strange and rich variety of other creatures including elves, goblins, dwarves, and, oh yes, humans. As you might expect, some of the creatures are good and peace-loving (hobbits, for example) and others are evil, menacing and downright terrifying (the Night Riders and Orcs to name just two).

8 The first film followed Frodo and his fellow-travellers. These included fellow hobbits, the wise wizard, Gandalf (McKellen), the human warrior, Aragorn (Mortensen), the elf, Legolas (Bloom) and Gimli, the dwarf (Rhys-Davies). The film ended with Gandalf disappearing into a fiery pit — presumably forever — and the troupe being split into three separate groups.

9 Be warned. *The Two Towers* film gives you no such history lesson. It simply shows Gandalf's descent into the pit, and then throws us straight into the action. And action aplenty there is too. If you thought *The Fellowship* too much of a boys-own-adventure kind of tale, don't worry about showing up for this one.

10 But the battle scenes are truly stupendous — certainly not for the faint-hearted, and certainly not for little ones. The baddies will bring back every nightmare you have ever had in your life, and then give you a few more.

11 This film follows the three traveller groups on their separate journeys — Frodo, his loyal chum Sam (Astin) and the previous owner of the ring, Gollum, in one; Aragorn, Legolas and Gimli in another; and Frodo's friends Pippin and Merry in the last. It takes more than the average degree of attention to follow the goings-on and keep up with all the new characters and new relationships. One criticism I did have in this regard is that quite often it was difficult to understand the dialogue — and in such a complex tale, you certainly need to hear every word.

12 I suppose I would have to agree with those who say that character development is not a strength of the Rings films. But there is one character in this film that blows away any criticism on this front — Gollum. Gollum may be computer-generated, but he sure involves our hearts and minds as he struggles between his good self (wanting to help Frodo) and his bad self (wanting the ring — his 'precious' — back in his own hands). A real actor (Serkis) played out all the scenes and then his performance was overlaid with computer graphics to create the tragic, twisted and pathetic character we see on the screen.

13 Still on character, I did think that the hobbit characters needed a bit more oomph. I am not sure if the fault lies with the script or the acting, but their roles, in this film anyway, did not go much beyond showing basic emotions — sad this moment, surprised the next, annoyed, scared and so on. It would be good to see a more complex show of character in the next film for each of them.

14 *The Two Towers* film is probably not as true to Tolkien's book as *The Fellowship*. Jackson has certainly moved the action away from the adventures of the gentle hobbits towards more traditional action heroes and battle scenes. Tolkien may not have been pleased. But the shift does not damage the film. *The Two Towers* is perhaps the most spectacular swashbuckler ever made. The computer animation and special effects are breathtaking, the real New Zealand scenery mouth-watering and the story and characters totally engaging as they play their part in the best kind of story of all — the battle of good against terrible and total evil.

15 A classic. Not to be missed.

UNDERSTANDING THE TEXT

1 If a star rating was used for the review (with 5 stars being the best), how many stars do you think the reviewer would give *The Two Towers*? ______________________

Give your reasons. ______________________

____

2 How many of the following aspects of film are mentioned by the reviewer? (Tick them.)

a ______ characters

b ______ plot

c ______ acting

d ______ visual effects

e ______ scenery

f ______ values reflected

g ______ direction

h ______ love scenes

i ______ script

j ______ comparison between book and film

k ______ level of violence

3 **a** What kind of films and characters does the reviewer usually like?

____

b Which of the following words best describes her reaction to the first film?

captivated interested unimpressed amused

c What is one of the *extraordinary odds* that Peter Jackson faced?

____

d Why does the reviewer tell the story of the *Fellowship of the Rings*?

____

e List the creatures mentioned who live in Middle Earth.

____

f What does the reviewer mean by *The Two Towers film gives you no such history lesson*?

____

g Why does the reviewer say the show is not for children?

____

h What criticism does the reviewer make in relation to following the story?

____

i Did the reviewer think the hobbit characters were the same in this film as in the last?

Which words tell you this? ______________________

j Does the reviewer think *The Two Towers* is **more** or **less** true to Tolkien's book than *The Fellowship of the Ring*? ______________________

4 Reviewers often use **colloquial** (conversational) language. This helps to make the tone personal, as though it were a dialogue between the reviewer and the reader only. What do these colloquial terms mean?

a first on the block (para 3) ______________________

b went for it (para 3) ______________________

c a quick recap (para 5) ______________________

d souls (para 5) ______________________

e downright (para 7) ______________________

f blows away (para 12) ______________________

g oomph (para 13) ______________________

5 Look at the words in italics in these sentences, and then tick the reviewer's meaning.

a 'Middle Earth is the world which the hobbits inhabit, along with a strange and rich variety of other creatures including elves, goblins, dwarves, and, *oh yes,* humans.'

______ There were definitely humans as well as non-human creatures in the film.

______ Amongst this strange world of non-human creatures it is easy to forget that there are humans as well.

b 'The film ended with Gandalf disappearing into a fiery pit — *presumably forever* — and the troupe being split into three separate groups.'

______ The reviewer is hinting that Gandalf might still be alive.

______ The reviewer presumes Gandalf is dead.

RESPONDING TO THE TEXT

1 Now that you have read the review, look back at your answer to Question **3** in Preparing to Read. Would you say the purpose of this review was mainly to inform, to entertain or to persuade? Give reasons.

____

____

2 If you have seen this film, do you agree with the reviewer? Why or why not? OR If you have not seen the film, would you like to having now read the review? Why or why not? (Write at least four sentences. Use your own paper.)

SPOTLIGHT ON LANGUAGE

Reviews usually include a range of descriptive vocabulary. Find these in the text (they are in the order they occur). Think of one other word you could use in their place. Use the dictionary if you need to.

rich	*complex*	*true to life*	*handsome*	*formidable*
epic	*remarkable*	*extraordinary*	*unimaginable*	*strange*
evil	*menacing*	*terrifying*	*stupendous*	*tragic*
twisted	*pathetic*	*traditional*	*spectacular*	*breathtaking*
mouth-watering	*engaging*			

The International Space Station

31

Webpage
Skimming
Distinguishing main ideas from supporting detail
Understanding complex sentences
Reading critically
Understanding word meanings

PREPARING TO READ

answers page 144

Skim the following text for 60 seconds. Then, without looking back, put a tick next to the topics you saw mentioned (not all are mentioned).

Milestones in space exploration	______	Countries involved in the space station	______
The first crew at the space station	______	Dimensions of the space station	______
Benefits for humankind	______	Construction of the space station	______
Daily life on the space station	______	How microgravity affects movement	______
Astronauts clothing	______	How to track the spacecraft from Earth	______

Now read the text carefully.

THE INTERNATIONAL SPACE STATION

NEWS & EVENTS | MISSIONS | MULTIMEDIA | EDUCATION

On October 4, 1957, the Russian satellite, Sputnik, rocketed into space and became the very first man-made object to break free of the Earth's orbit. Many space exploration milestones have been achieved since then, including the first man in space in 1961, the first space walk in 1965, first man on the Moon in 1969, the first landing on Mars in 1976, and the first space shuttle in 1981. After these came various explorer vessels which have travelled the solar system, reporting back to us on the mysterious world that we inhabit. 1

Now at the beginning of the 21st century we have a new landmark achievement in process — the development of the International Space Station (ISS). The ISS is a remarkable achievement in more ways than one. Not only is it a miracle of scientific and technological know-how, but it is also a monument to international cooperation. 2

The ISS is a joint venture between the USA, Russia, Japan, Canada, Brazil and the 15 nations of the European Space Agency — Belgium, Britain, Ireland, Portugal, Austria, Denmark, France, Germany, Italy, the Netherlands, Norway, Spain, Finland, Sweden and Switzerland. The collaboration of the US and Russia is extraordinary in itself, given the fact that up until the end of the Cold War, these two countries were bitter rivals in the superpower 'space race'. 3

A truly amazing aspect of the ISS is that it is being constructed in space. This makes it the largest, most ambitious construction project humankind has ever attempted — and the most expensive. Current estimates of cost are around the $120 billion mark. It will be 88.4 metres long and have a wingspan of 108.5 metres. It will have six solar-powered laboratories and other components for living quarters, command and control, storage and so on. It will also have a Robonaut, a robot with a robotic arm that will assemble and repair parts of the station's exterior. Most construction, however, is done by live astronauts. To build the station, they must perform highly dangerous space-walks along its exterior connecting equipment and doing maintenance and repair tasks. **4**

When complete, the ISS will be like a little city in the space. It will orbit 407 kilometres above the Earth, take 90 minutes to do a complete orbit at an average speed of 28,000 kilometres an hour, and circle the Earth sixteen times a day. It will be the third brightest object in the sky after the Sun and the Moon. It will be a place where scientists from all over the world will be able to live and study for long periods of time — and most importantly — in a weightless environment (microgravity). This will be an unprecedented opportunity, and will lead to a better understanding of gravity's effects on all living things on earth. Microgravity will allow scientists to do experiments that are impossible on Earth, blending and creating substances that may lead to treatments for diseases like cancer and AIDS, for example. Scientists believe that new products and inventions will result from developments aboard the station. The mechanism developed for the Robonaut, for example, is seen to have great potential for amputees on Earth. **5**

The space station will also be a step towards further space exploration. It will allow scientists to investigate solutions for long-term space travel, essential if we are ever going to travel to Mars or other planets. It will also help us to understand our own planet because for the first time we will be able to have a permanent platform from which to observe it over long periods. **6**

The ISS is due to be completed in 2006 although delays so far make it unlikely that this target will be achieved. The Columbia disaster in 2003 has been a major setback to the program because of the space station's dependence on the US space shuttles. This tragic incident also caused people to question the value of risking lives to explore space — and not for the first time. The same uncertainty followed the Challenger disaster of 1986. Nevertheless, it seems certain that space exploration will continue. It seems certain, too, that sometime in the next few years we will be able to look up to the stars and see evidence that fellow human beings have got the lights switched on, and are up and about working hard for the benefit of us all. **7**

Life on board the ISS

Life is pretty busy for the astronauts on the ISS. The first job each day is to make sure that all systems are working as they should. Then it's breakfast time. In past space missions, spacefood was always freeze-dried, and so fairly bland and boring. The space station, however, has microwaves and refrigerators, so the food is more like what we might have at home. Astronauts eat together around the dining table as this is thought to be important psychologically. The rest of the day is spent working (12 hours) and exercising (2 hours) with breaks for other meals, and then sleep (8.5 hours). — with astronauts securely tied down to their beds so they don't just float away. **8**

Spare time is very brief and astronauts spend it just like you or me — reading, listening to CDs, or looking out the window (not a bad view). Exercise is an extremely important part of the day. Microgravity can cause muscles and bones to weaken and atrophy, so regular exercise is vital for health while on board and for when astronauts return to Earth. Personal hygiene is a little challenging in space. Washing is done using water recycled from the water vapour given off by every living thing on board (laboratory rats included), and flowing air instead of water removes waste from the toilet. **9**

UNDERSTANDING THE TEXT

1 The purpose of the text is to: (circle one)

- **a** describe the ISS and explain its purpose.
- **b** compare the ISS to previous space projects.
- **c** explain how the ISS was built.
- **d** argue the case for space exploration.

2 All these ideas are in the text. Write **M** if the idea is a main idea. Write **S** if it is a detail that supports a main idea.

- **a** The ISS is a remarkable achievement in international cooperation. ______
- **b** Exercise is an important part of the day. ______
- **c** The ISS follows many other landmark achievements in space. ______
- **d** The ISS will cost around $120 billion. ______
- **e** Scientists will be able to do experiments that they cannot do on Earth. ______
- **f** The first man-made object to go into space was the Sputnik. ______
- **g** The astronauts have a very busy life on board the ISS. ______
- **h** The ISS is a remarkable scientific and technological achievement. ______
- **i** The ISS will be a very significant place for research. ______
- **j** It is extraordinary that the US and Russia are working together on this project. ______

3 Answer these questions in your own words.

- **a** Why is it extraordinary that the United States and Russia are working together?

  ____

- **b** In what particular way is the ISS the most ambitious project humankind has attempted?

  ____

- **c** What is so very important about the ISS environment for research?

  ____

- **d** How will the ISS help us understand our planet better?

  ____

- **e** Is the ISS expected to finish on time? ______________________

- **f** Why is exercise so important for the astronauts?

  ____

4 The words on the left below are from the text. Find them and read again the sentences before and after. Then choose the word on the right which best matches the meaning in the context.

a	**monument to** (para 2)	building erected to	important example of
b	**joint venture** (para 3)	combined effort	common place
c	**collaboration** (para 3)	cooperation	attitude
d	**unprecedented** (para 5)	excellent	never known or done before
e	**potential** (para 5)	possibilities	invention
f	**setback** (para 7)	step backwards	settling
g	**atrophy** (box)	hurt	waste away

5 Even when a text is *information*-focused, it is important to think about how the writer's views might have affected which information is included in the text and which is left out. Answer these questions.

a Is it possible for two people to have differing views on space exploration? Why / why not?

____

____

b Do you think the writer is for or against space exploration? ____________________

c What makes you think this (give examples of words used or information included)?

____

____

d What negative points are included about the ISS or space exploration in general?

____

e Can you think of any negative aspects of space exploration that the writer should have mentioned more about?

____

RESPONDING TO THE TEXT

1 The last line says the ISS astronauts are *working hard for the benefit of us all*. Do *you* think that the ISS will benefit us all? Do you think so much money should be spent on the ISS? Write a paragraph giving your view, using information from the text or elsewhere. (Use your own paper.)

2 Use the Internet to find information about the International Space Station — track where it is, find out which construction stage it is up to, and which crew is in residence.

ANSWERS

PART ONE: KEY READING SKILLS

1 Skimming for gist or preview — Page 4

1 **a** Bridge Miracle **b** Mountain Fall **c** More Beach Closures **d** Counterfeit Alert **e** Race Smash **f** Explosives Find

2 **a** Kissing began when cavemen began licking their neighbours' cheeks for the salt on them **b** Western countries **c** Possible answers: Any examples from paragraph 2 **d** any examples from paragraph 3 **e** any examples from paragraph 4 **f** on the increase.

2 Scanning for specific information — Page 8

1 **a** between 10 am and 12 noon, Saturday **b** 12.30 pm, Saturday **c** 11.30am to 12.30 pm, Sunday **d** Greens Road **e** 2 pm, Saturday **f** 2 pm, Sunday, in the car park behind the railway station **g** Centre stage **h** 11.30 am to 12.30 pm, Saturday **i** 2.30 to **3**pm, Sunday **j** From 3pm to 8 pm, Saturday, and from 3pm to 6pm, Sunday

2 **a** 3 – red wolf, Asiatic cheetah, and Northern hairy-nosed Wombat **b** 4 – Indian, Ceylon, Sumatra and Malaysian elephants **c** less than 50 mature animals **d** by at least 50% **e** South America only **f** less than 250 mature animals **g** Iran **h** Continuing erosion of habitat as forests have been cut down for settlement and agriculture **i** 8

3 Predicting — Page 12

1 The text is most probably about **b** (the risks of skateboarding for children).

2 The Chapter is about how some animals can camouflage themselves by, for example, changing their colour.

3 The most probable matches are: **a** iii **b** ii **c** iv **d** v **e** i

4 A young surfer has escaped unscathed after a three-metre shark repeatedly attacked his surfboard taking a large chunk out of it. Michael Brown, 17, was surfing with two friends off Scotchy Head, when the shark, probably a bronze whaler, attacked about 6.30 am Sunday. It charged his board, throwing him into the air. The youth regained the board, but as he and his friends struggled to catch a wave back to shore, the shark attacked again, biting a large chunk out of it. The three managed to reach the beach unhurt. Later that day the boys were relaxing at home with family and friends, enjoying being the centre of attention for the day. However, they warned all surfers to take special care when surfing: 'Just because shark attacks are rare, doesn't mean they don't ever happen,' said Michael. The three friends also stressed the need to surf with your mates. 'It is just stupid to go out alone,' said Michael.

5 No answers needed. Here is the complete text, however, for you to see.
People can try to interpret their dreams. But to do that one has to remember them, and most dreams vanish before the end of the morning first's yawn. Some dream experts suggest putting a pen and paper by your bed. As soon as you wake, you should write down any recollections before you do anything.

6 No answers needed. Here is the complete text, however, for you to see.
To interpret what your dream meant, think about the area of your life the dream was about. In general, we dream about things that are relevant to our own experiences. Experts warn that we should not be frightened of our dreams. They are not instructions, just insights. What we do with the information is up to us.

4 Working out word meanings — Page 16

1 wheel

2 A ringing mobile phone gave away the *hiding* place of a man who had allegedly *assaulted* a female police officer yesterday. Police said the 23-year-old man *stole* a cash box from the front *office* of a caravan park at Adelie Beach on the North Coast. He then *allegedly* pushed the officer to the *ground* after she asked him what he was *doing*, and fled on *foot* into thick bushland behind the beach A second *officer* gave chase but lost *sight* of the suspect. Then the officer heard a mobile phone *ringing* quite nearby. He followed the *sound* and found the man *hiding* behind a large rock The man was arrested and *charged* with stealing, assault, and resisting arrest and will *appear* in Portland Court on March 12.

3 **a** i **b** ii **c** iii **d** i **e** i

4 **a** body positions **b** captured and held in zoos or similar places **c** used to **d** useful in many different ways **e** makes sound louder **f** copying **g** think it is likely, hypothesise **h** specific or peculiar to one animal **i** pushed together and forward

5 Understanding writer's purpose and organisation Page 19

1 **a** iii

b

	Spiders	Insects
Similarities	look alike are invertebrates belong to arthropods have exoskeletons have segmented bodies have jointed limbs can bite and sting	
Differences	body in two sections four pairs of walking legs simple eyes (six to eight) no antennae or wings silk glands in abdomen spinnerets to weave webs no true jaws — feed with sucking action after poisoning prey	body in three sections three pairs of walking legs compound eyes and simple eyes antennae and wings no silk glands no spinnerets true jaws

2 **a** i

b

3 **a** ii

b Sample answer:

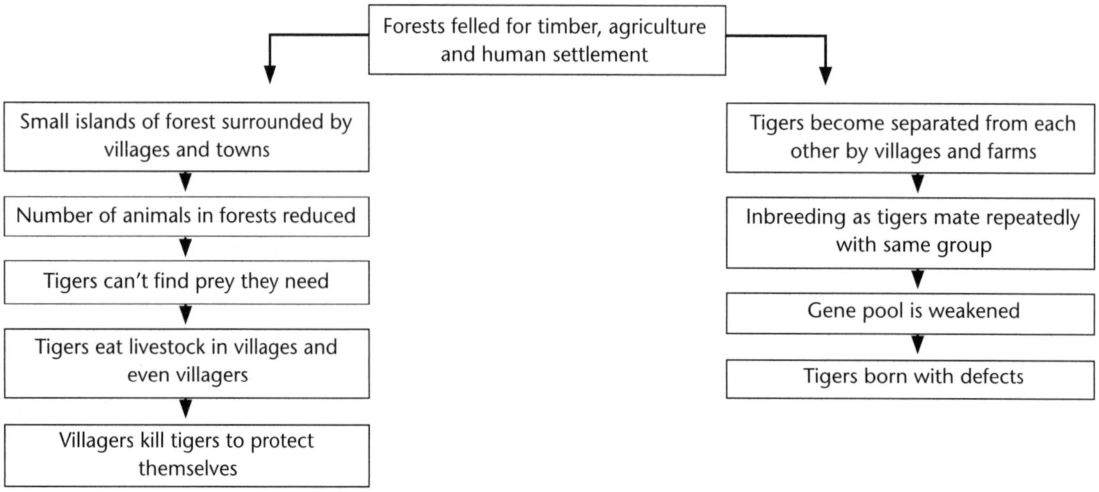

The correct order for sentences is shown below:
d Art in the form of graffiti originated in the late 1960s, though graffiti in the form of words or drawings scratched on walls to
express an idea had been around for a long time before then.
b Around that time, the words 'Julio 204' began appearing all around New York city.
a Julio's tag was quickly followed by 'Taki 183' which turned out to be the tag of a young Manhattan man called Demetrius.
e In 1971, the New York Times found and interviewed Taki 183 to try and explain the new phenomenon.
c Within a year of the article on Taki 183 appearing, hundreds of new writers emerged and took New York City by storm.

6 Understanding main ideas

Page 23

1 **a** **i** 2 Your skin is waterproof.
ii 1 Your skin is an all-purpose covering.
iii 4 Your insides need to be kept moist so that they don't stop working.
iv 3 Skin keeps water out, and more importantly, it keeps water in.

b **i** 1 Our faces are windows into our thoughts and feelings.
ii 2 Something in our faces signals whether, for example, we are lying or not.
iii 4 The psychologist travelled the world looking at faces in all kinds of culture.
iv 3 One US psychologist set out to discover the rules that govern how we interpret facial expressions.

2 **a** 2 *This* is not surprising given that when we are frightened or upset our heart starts thumping.
b 5 *Today we know* that the heart is just a muscular pump for the blood.
c 4 *But* the belief turned out to be wrong.
d 1 *In the past*, people used to think that the heart controlled the whole body including feelings and emotions.
e 7 *What is more,* we know that the whole body is controlled by this amazing organ.
f 3 *This* old belief gave rise to phrases like 'I know it in my heart'.
g 6 *We know* that the heart is in fact controlled by the brain.

3 **a** 4 *Two in three, for example,* would talk to their mothers about failing exams whereas one in three would talk to their fathers.
b 1 *A recent study* of Australian youth has some good news for mothers around the country.
c 5 *And* more than half would tell mum if they were worried about something while only one-quarter would tell dad.
d 3 *Mothers* were nominated *more than twice* as often as fathers *overall* as the person they would talk to.
e 2 *The survey* of 400 young people between 8 and 15 showed that young people think that *mother*s are better than fathers to talk to about most topics.

4 Missing words shown in italics:
Laughter is part of human *behaviour* all over the world, yet it not very well *understood.* We laugh for a variety of *reasons,* not only because we find something *funny/humorous*. One recent study set out to discover how we develop our sense of humour, and expected to find that it was to do with our *genes* not our upbringing. The study tested the responses of fraternal and *identical* twins to a set of cartoons. They found that twins in *both* groups tended to have similar views as their siblings about what was funny. The interesting thing was that the *identical* twins were no more likely to agree than the *fraternal* twins. This suggests that shared genes played no part but shared *upbringing* did. The surprising results might explain the cultural *differences* in senses of humour.

5 **a** **i** S **ii** M **iii** S **iv** S **v** M **vi** S **vii** M **viii** S **ix** S **x** M

b Main idea best expressed by **x**. The title including the word 'epidemic' reflects the important point that kissing is on the increase. The whole text, including all the other main points, builds up to this important one.

7 Understanding detail

Page 28

1 **a** therefore, because of this **b** information about religion and government
c hieroglyphics **d** Egyptian scribes

2 **a** true records **b** accurate **c** records of historical events or the actions or rulers not being accurate

3 **a** 4th century AD **b** July 1799 **c** a French soldier **d** He was at a French fort established by Napoleon's army. **e** three **f** Greek **g** One of the scripts looked like hieroglyphics, and another was in Greek. They thought this might help to discover what the hieroglyphics meant. **h** The Rosetta Stone

i to honour the Egyptian Pharoah of the time. **j** The benefits the Pharoah had given to Egypt. **k** about 20 years **l** A Frenchman, Jean-Francois Champollion, 14 years. **m** Thomas Young's

4 The questions about the most important ideas are probably: **g**, **h**, **i**, **l**.

5 **a** makes us less stressed, lowers our blood pressure, reduces anxiety
b any examples from paragraph 2 **c** keep conversations going, make people feel part of a group
d our sense of humour had more to do with our genes than our upbringing **e** by our genes **f** 56
g Gary Larson's **h** True **i** True

8 Understanding complex sentences Page 33

1 Main clauses are shown below:
a Radio can report on events **b** radio can often be first with the news. **c** Radio can abandon all its other programs **d** In bushfire disasters, radio informs people about the location of fires **e** almost every radio station in the country incorporates a talkback segment

2 Sentence subjects are shown below:
a programs **b** programs **c** stories **d** example **e** competition **f** programs

3 Possible answers:
a With newspapers / it is possible / to flick through the pages, / scan the headlines / and the introductory paragraphs, / read an article on one page / and then go back / and read another report / in a different part of the paper.
b The newsreader's job / is to introduce the news item / and make it possible / for a journalist / to continue it with film / that has been selected.
c The limited time for in-depth treatment of stories in the TV news / means that TV viewers / do not get as much detail / as newspaper readers.
d Natural-sounding speech / helps to create an impression / that the newsreader and journalists / are having a conversation with each viewer / rather than talking to millions of viewers / in a million different lounge rooms / all at once

9 Understanding graphs and tables Page 36

1 **a** 1999 and 2001 **b** No **c** 88% **d** more, 21%; **e** the number of 10–17 year olds who had an email address in 2001 **f** 4% **g** increase **h** your own answer

2 **a** 13 including 'other' **b** what teenagers use the internet for and what they use it for most **c** as a study resource **d** for news and weather **e** 30% **f** 14% **g** 45% **h** true **i** your own answer.

3 **a** true **b** not clear **c** true **d** soccer and skateboarding **e** soccer **f** 28% **g** increase **h** <u>either</u> that girls don't play as much sport as boys, <u>or</u> that there is no one single girls' sport that has as many participants as these four boys' sports **i** your own answer

4 **a** Soccer **b** 19.6% **c** netball **d** 18.2% **e** yes (2500) **f** yes (6400) **g** athletics **h** the number of boys and girls who played Australian Rules football **i** the results differ in that firstly the table includes popular girls' sports such as netball; secondly, the table shows that Australian Rules football, tennis, swimming and basketball are more popular boys sports than Rugby League **j** These results might differ because firstly, the research which led to the first graph might not have included girls; secondly, the graph research may not have included question about these sports, and it might have been done mainly in areas where Rugby League was the main football game.

10 Inferring Page 41

1 **a** Jacko and Toby
b perhaps a few weeks — long enough for Jacko's growl to be familiar but not long enough to considered a permanent home – he and Toby are sleeping on mattresses **c** grumpy, angry, discontent – the words *heavy footsteps, a shouting of voices,* the *growl* and *slammed shut.*
d usual because the growl is familiar to Michael
e an uncared for, bare room in a house or flat — the words *the bare boards of the hallway, the thin blanket, cracked glass, curtainless window, mattress*
f He is probably in trouble of some kind, perhaps he has been thrown out of home, perhaps he is hiding from someone, e.g. the police, a gang member.

2 **a** in a small town. It sounds like the school is on the street next to the beach, and also she feels very much that the people on the street would look at her because she is a stranger. This makes 'a small town' more likely than 'a city suburb'. It is clearly not 'a deserted bit of coast' because other people and the street are mentioned.

b Afternoon. She is walking home at the same time as other kids, so it is probably just after school time.

c Unhappy. She feels drawn to a sea eagle more than the other kids, she wants to be by herself and *in peace.*

d Has recently moved to the area. She seems to be attending school so she must live there, but the people are strangers so she must not have lived there for long.

3 **a** At school. Her open exercise book, the HB pencil, Pam's two hours' of work, the mention of Annabel.

b Quite serious, hard-working. She has worked hard to draw her map and is upset that is destroyed.

c It is raining heavily. The water is coming through the ceiling.

d Pam is a little unsure about Annabel's friendship. She tells herself that Annabel must not have seen what happened in order to explain to herself why Annabel could smile at this moment. But she can't smile back properly, only *thinly*. Also *smiling sugar* suggests that Annabel's smile might not be genuine.

e Pam seems especially upset about her work being destroyed – she *throttled* the pencil and had to stop herself from throwing the book away; she *glared* at the ceiling and *dared* it to drop another *bomb*. These extreme reactions suggest she might be upset or unhappy about something else also. The part about Annabel suggests that all is not well with that relationship, so it might be that, or perhaps it is the heavy rain and what damage that might be causing.

4 **a** The words *beyond recovery* suggest that no-one is trying to recover them now.

b Australian scientists don't want the Great Barrier Reef to be destroyed so we can assume that they are doing something to stop that happening.

c The word *unfortunately* suggests that the writer is unhappy about the situation, and would want the reef to be saved.

d The reef gets *run-off* from sugar farms so they must be somewhere near the coast.

e The fish, corals and sea animals are the very things the tourists come to see, so we can assume they will not come if those things are not there to be seen.

11 Reading critically — Page 46

1 **a** Street artists consider trains and streets as a gallery for their artwork. (+)

b All concerned citizens will surely support the anti-graffiti squad in their fight against graffiti crime. (-)

c Urban artists have decorated the wall by the local railway station. (+)

d We need to take action against these criminals head-on. (-)

e The battle against graffiti terrorists is on. (-)

f Graffiti vandals should be made to confront their victims. (-)

g Graffiti websites showcase the colourful and creative work of aerosol artists. (+)

h These hoons aren't the ones who have to clean up their mess. (-)

i Young people who do graffiti may not have any other opportunity to express their artistic ideas. (+)

j One concerned gentleman at the anti-graffiti meeting suggested residents adopt an area to keep watch for graffiti vandalism. (-)

k The young artists thanked the Mayor for the opportunity to do a graffiti mural at the community centre. (+)

2 **a** F **b** F **c** F **d** O **e** F (It is fact that the book *claims* we are not alone. It may, however, be mostly opinion that is expressed in the book.) **f** O **g** F **h** O **i** F

3 **a** **i** Fact **ii** no right or wrong answer, but because the paragraph is factual we might predict that an information text will follow.

b *useful*

c **i** Opinion, because it is about the future. **ii** 7 sentences about positive outcomes **iii** two sentences about negative outcomes. **iv** The writer should perhaps have written more about the negative outcomes to appear more balanced. Another negative outcome might be warfare between planets, and even occupation or destruction of our planet. **v** *This could only be to our benefit; extraordinary opportunity*

d **i** Two lines given to lack of evidence **ii** Fact **iii** Over 4 lines given to the possibility of life **iv** opinion **v** This tells us that the writer is probably a big supporter of the search for extra-terrestrial life — he emphasises the positive and downplays the negative.

e **i** Opinion. **ii** If there are many scientists searching for SETI, then no government would be able to cover up any findings.

f The reader might feel they were a little stupid if they were not fascinated by SETI, and so might think they should find out more about it. This is likely to be the effect the writer wants.

PART TWO: READING TEXTS

Note: Sometimes there are no answers given. This is usually in the **Preparing to read** or **Responding to the text** sections where the answers are your own predictions or ideas.

12 Newsworthiness — Page 52

Preparing to read

1 **b** to explain how journalists and editors select news stories

Understanding the text

1 **c** explains the idea in the topic sentence and gives examples

2 **a** para 2, conflict **b** para 7, newspapers **c** para 3, crime **d** para 5, achievements **e** para 7, away

3 **a** … will interest the majority of readers.
b … the conflict led to extreme violence.
c … the home country is involved in some way.
d … unusual …
e … make us feel lucky not to be affected, and they make us feel good to be humans when we hear of people doing good things for victims, even risking their lives.
f … a story about outstanding feats.

4 **a** feats **b** ultimate **c** avidly **d** applaud **e** grim **f** intrigue

13 Never say die — Page 56

Preparing to read

1 There is no right answer because you are predicting only, but the introduction suggests that the text contains stories of people who have survived life-threatening situations.

2 Your skimming should confirm the above answer.

Understanding the text

1 **a** True **b** False **c** False **d** True **e** False **f** True **g** True **h** False **i** True **j** False

2 **a** She was on the river to search for an Aboriginal rock site.

b She made her way to a steep mud slope aiming to pull herself up on the low branch of a paperbark tree.

c The crocodile rolling with the victim under the water. (You can work this out from the paragraph.)

d By dragging herself and crawling.

e Because they are quoted from the story she wrote for the *Quadrant* magazine.

3 **a** threatening **b** moved forward suddenly **c** with great energy and speed **d** not wanting to believe **e** pulled with force **f** quick thinking **g** scratching and scraping **h** a clump of short grass **i** put up with for a long time **j** idea/situation hard to understand because it contains opposing facts

Spotlight on language

Other examples of powerful verbs to describe the action in the text are: seized, whirled (para 3); grabbed, propelled, seized, wrenched (para 4); rammed, heaving, flung, scrabbling, grabbed, pushed, haul (para 5); dragged, staggering (para 6); catapulted (para 7).

14 Contact — Part One Page 60

Preparing to read

1 She is flying a plane.

2 Alone, and nervous because of how difficult it is going to be to land the plane.

3 There is no right answer because you are predicting, but **a** is perhaps a more likely answer than **b** or **c**. The first two paragraphs are focused on what has happened and what is happening, so you expect this to continue. You might expect to find out about the woman's background, **b**, or to get an explanation of how she came to be in the situation, **c**, later in the story but probably not for a few pages. However, stories do sometimes begin with an account of action and then move backwards in time to explain something about the situation or the characters, so if you chose **b** or **c**, and justified it in this way, this would also be an acceptable answer.

Understanding the text

1 1 She slowed the aircraft because of the mountains.
2 She saw a town in the valley.
3 Snowclouds first touched the plane.
4 She flew around the forest.
5 Snow fell on the plane.
6 She saw chimney smoke.

2 **a** being chased. Phrases that paint this picture: *she glanced quickly over her shoulder, hadn't a hope of outrunning them* [the clouds], *terrifying body massed behind*

3 **a** *Wraith* can mean a visible spirit of a dead person, or something pale and transparent (like a spirit), like vapour or smoke.
b The writer probably intends us to get an image of the snowclouds as something ghostly, pale and transparent (and so quite threatening), but with one part protruding from the mass like a finger or hand. There is a sense that the clouds are alive.
c *wraith-finger, terrifying body, coiled over*

4 **a** landform **b** bare and windswept **c** part of the plane over the pilot's head **d** disturbing **e** turned **f** with bitter amusement **g** airy and light **h** distant and isolated **i** nothing more than **j** interrupting

5 **a** future (the mention of some remote places still using overhead powerlines suggests the future. Overhead powerlines are still very common today.)
b unfriendly (*houses enclosed by high timber fences that sealed them completely from outsiders*)
c very different (Mahla would probably be one of the *outsiders*)

15 Contact — Part Two Page 64

Understanding the text

1 **a** She usually likes it (she finds the different tones and shades *friendly*). **b** She feels very uncomfortable (it is all one tone and this is *suffocating*). **c** Because when she goes slow, she does not have so much control of the craft. Also a warning signal goes off and the sound of it disturbs her. (Look back to paragraph 2 in Part One for the first mention of the slow speed indicator.) **d** The noise of the airspeed indicator. **e** They had raised footpaths on either side which created a deep channel in the middle. **f** She wanted to use the fence as a windbreak and as a line which would help her keep straight (a line of sight). **g** Standing and stepping out of the craft (because of the force of the wind). **h** The gates opened by themselves with the force of the wind. **i** The gate hitting into and damaging her plane. **j** She was hit by one gate panel down the side of her body and thrown into the air by the force. She landed (still standing) on the opposite side of the road next to the fence. She dropped to the ground and lost consciousness.

3 **a** swirl or eddy **b** desperation **c** freak **d** dauntingly **e** lashed **f** flexed **g** bulged

Spotlight on language

Positive sound words: unbroken shush, steady hum, sound of the air, purr of the engine

Negative sound words: shrilled, screamed, screaming, agonised shriek, insane howling of the wind, fearful grinding

The questions are asked by Mahla. She is asking herself these questions. They make us feel we are with her, even inside her head.

16 Cannibalism in animals

Page 68

Understanding the text

1

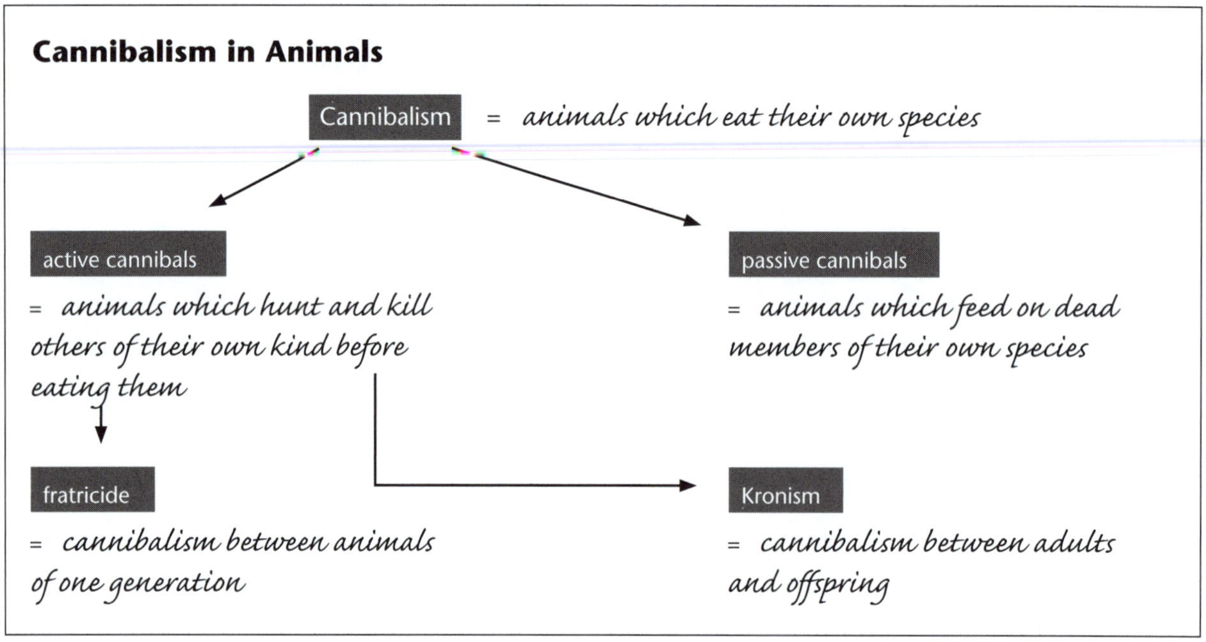

2 **a** False **b** True **c** Keeping the population numbers down and so not eliminating the food supply. **d** True **e** False **f** To protect their own offspring. **f** Infanticide, because the lions generally do not eat the cubs they kill. **h** Female lions reproduce very slowly, and males have a breeding period of only about three years (so there is not much opportunity to father cubs.

3 **a** widespread **b** greedily, quickly or in great quantities **c** control or restriction **d** while damaging **e** characteristic **f** death rate **g** in addition **h** extremely important

Spotlight on language

cannibalism (noun), cannibal (noun), cannibalistic (adjective), cannibalise (verb)

predatory (adjective), prey (noun), predator (noun)

17 Pocket money tops $50

Page 72

Preparing to read

1 That many 14 year olds and even 10 year olds get $50 pocket money.

Understanding the text

1 **a** 45% **b** none at all **c** 1% **d** 5% **e** none at all **f** children who get pocket money (46% get none, but 54% — total of all the other percentages — *do* get pocket money)

2 **a** Not very accurate, seeing that only 1% of 10 year olds and 5% of 14 year olds get $50 or more pocket money. **b** The headline is written like this to attract the readers' attention and get them to read the article. Most people would be surprised to read that many children get $50 pocket money, and so would be interested in reading more about it. They would not be very surprised to read that most 10 year olds, for example, get no pocket money, or usually get less than $10, and so might not even read the article. (Note: headlines are often written by a different journalist – that is, not the journalist who wrote the article — their job is to pick up something in the article that will most attract readers.)

3 **a** Quantum Market Research **b** four **c** One hundred 10–11 year olds were surveyed **d** See **2b** **e** No, because her two children would use it differently, and this might cause problems **f** Yes, because it teaches them the value of money **g** Because she is a clinical psychologist who works with children and so her opinion on the issue is considered valuable **h** She thinks it is beneficial but thinks it is important for parents to be balanced about it — not too much and not too little.

4

Information about research method	**Stated explicitly (directly)**	**Can be inferred (worked out)**	**Not stated explicitly or able to be inferred**
What question/questions were asked		√ (We can work out children were asked 'How much pocket money do you get each week?'	
How the information was obtained (e.g. written survey, interview)	√ (It says in the article that one 10 year old ticked the box so we know it was a written survey)		
How many children were surveyed		√ (We can work it out from detail in article about one 10 year old ticking the $50 and over box – see 3c)	
Where children lived (e.g. city, country)			√

b If we knew where the survey was done we could be more confident about the results. The survey was probably done across the country, but, if it was not (for example, it was only done with city children), then this would be important to know.

18 How science began to solve crime — Page 75

Understanding the text

1 **a** after **b** after **c** during **d** during **e** before

2 **a**

3 **a** mainly looking for suspects. **b** a person to blame. **c** it was a good idea to use thought and reasoning to solve crime. **d** the 1800s. **e** a simple idea but complex in practice. **f** the measurements of the head and fingers first. **g** slowly.

4 **a** someone to blame **b** using clues to solve crime **c** a forensic method using body measurements of arrested criminals **d** wrongly identifying someone **e** not very easy to use **f** non-believers

19 Life on the edge — Page 78

Preparing to read

c

Understanding the text

1 **a** Frightened and sick; the word *grey-faced* **b** The writer; she says it is a *novice* (first-time) jumper; she describes what is going on in her head. **c** She means going back to a time when she was completely safe and was cared for completely by her mother (and not facing danger like this). **d** Examples of everyday boring things in most people's lives. **e** To show the difference between these things and skydiving. **f** She is saying that she understands completely why no-one would come back for a second time (it is so scary). **g** She wants to know how he is feeling today because she is putting her life in his hands. **h** Because this increases the odds of her dive being the one to go wrong.

2 The first set of words conveys a sense of falling terrifyingly fast through the air without the parachute — she uses short and harsh consonant sounds to do this, e.g. (*plummeting, chin flapping, sick*). The second set conveys the slow, gentle, floating feeling once the parachute opens — she uses soft sounds and words that take longer to say (e.g. *floating-above-the-earth, human-turned-into-butterfly, leaf-floating-on-air-current*).

3 No one right answer, but perhaps **d** is most likely. The writer writes mostly about her fear, but shows, at the end, that she was pleased she did it.

20 Tapioca to the rescue — Page 82

Preparing to read

b

Understanding the text

1 **a** a racing car driver **b** a racing car driver **c** policy director of Australian Retailers Association **d** head of PlanetArk, an environmental group **e** Environment Minister

Least important: Craig Lowndes and Mark Skaife

2 **a** Aldi stores **b** Bangladesh Government **c** BP stores **d** South African Government **e** Irish government **f** PlanetArk **g** Australian government **h** Australian Retailers Association

3 **a** False **b** True **c** False **d** True

4 The article outlines different ways that governments have tried to overcome the problem of plastic bags, and describes a bag made from tapioca which is being trialled by the environmental group PlanetArk.

5 **a** solve a problem **b** might not complete a task or get to a place **c** been criticised **d** follow an example **e** introduced a heavy payment or tax **f** treasury or bank of money **g** taken the first steps, shown the way **h** named

Spotlight on language

The very short paragraphs make it look like it is not a difficult or heavy article to read.

The use of interesting or amusing information at the start is to get the reader into the story and to link it to something they might know.

The use of the headline which is at first difficult to understand is to intrigue the reader and make them read on – to find the explanation for the headline.

21 Night of Passage — Part One — Page 86

Preparing to read

a girl **b** fantasy world **c** a journey

Understanding the text

1 Brin was travelling on her own — para 1

Brin's journey was something she had to do to become a woman — para 5

Brin is close to her family — para 8

Brin would be in some danger on her journey — para 2, 3 or 4

Brin feels very alone — para 7

Brin lived in a country area — para 3

Brin wanted to complete the journey even though she was afraid — para 5 or 7

Brin was not the first to do this journey – para 2, 5 or 10

2 **a** lithe **b** labyrinth **c** wafted **d** gaunt **e** wan **f** loomed **g** discreet **h** inkling **i** rime

3 **a** went a long way in a short time, covered a distance in less time than expected

b the journey would be more difficult

c would wait for a better time to take an action

d would make her harder to be seen

e trusted to be told secrets

f to look around and assess the situation

g caused her to make

h went ahead of her (she could sense things before she saw them)

i avoided these things

j she had done this kind of thing before

4 *predators on this no-man's land, littered relics of the old ones; ruins of an ancient wheeled vehicle* especially suggest that a war has taken place. Generally there is a suggestion that Brin is travelling in an area that is abandoned because of something bad that has happened at an earlier time.

22 Night of Passage — Part Two   Page 90

Understanding the text

1 **a** the light of heaven **b** the centre of the city **c** the buildings **d** staying close to the buildings and their shadows so that she could not be seen **e** the fear and anxiety of those young people who had completed the ritual and survived to tell the story
f about the presence of wild dogs

2 **a** She needs to prove that she has reached the centre of the city. A trophy is an object she could take back which proved this.

b She says that the homes of her people *blended harmoniously with their surroundings* and dislikes the city buildings, which are so different.

c She pushed away her fears and forced herself to be strong (like steel) and do what she had to.

d Yes. The text says: *even now … it was known that the city was not entirely deserted*; Brin had heard strange stories from those who had come back from the city; and, many young people had not come back, suggesting that they had been killed or taken hostage.

e *initiates*; initial, initiate (all have meaning of 'first' or 'first time').

f Because she suspects that some stories were made up and exaggerated by the fears and anxieties of the story-tellers.

g That wild dogs prowled the city; that these dogs would be more dangerous than those in the country areas.

h This term means getting to (attaining) the age at which you are considered an adult in your society. In many Western countries this is considered to be the age of 21. In Brin's society it was not an age but the successful completion of the journey which was important.

i It would make her braver (*shore up her courage*).

j She hears the sorrowful howl of an animal. It makes her afraid (*her scalp prickled with apprehension*).

3 **a** P, good, favourable **b** N, bare, plain, without decoration **c** N, short and wide **d** N, making a sound like metal hitting metal **e** N, an unpleasant sound made from a group of sounds **f** P, sounds blending together in a good way **g** N, waited in hiding with evil intentions **h** N, deeply sad **i** N, fear about what is to come **j** N, very sad, unable to be consoled

Spotlight on language

Sample answers: This was what her trial was all about; She was looking forward to sharing tales with him when he became a man; and leave quickly before daylight came; She entered the city making sure that she could not be seen.

23 Rap music — the beginnings   Page 94

Understanding the text

1 **a** gifted teenagers in the South Bronx **b** hip-hop **c** how young people (mainly African and Caribbean Americans) responded in a creative way to their neglected, poor environment. **d** They danced and they painted. **e** False **f** disco, rhythm and blues, soul and funk **g** Manipulating records as they played and creating new songs with long instrumental breaks **h** beat, break or Bronx **i** dance, fight **j** True **k** white musicians beginning to sing in rap style **l** political and 'gangsta' rap, because of the language and attitudes in these songs **m** False

2 para 1: Born in the ghetto; para 2: What the terms mean; para 3: Influences and techniques; para 4: A new kind of dancing; para 5: Into the mainstream; para 6: A major musical influence

3 **a** forge **b** ingenuity **c** chronicling **d** interchangeably **e** cherish **f** monopolising **g** fringes

4 **a** from the old things they had around the place **b** burning hot, strong and intense **c** the neighbourhood **d** powered with

24 Human cloning Page 98

Understanding the text

1 Letter 1 **F/D**; Letter 2 **F**; Letter 3 **F**; Letter 4 **A**; Letter 5 **D**; Letter 6 **A**; Letter 7 **F**; Letter 8 **A**

2 **a** Letter 1 **b** Letter 3 **c** Letter 8 **d** Letter 6 **e** Letter 5 **f** Letter 2 **g** Letter 4 **h** Letter 7

3 **a** Letter 1 **O**; Letter 2 **O**; Letter 3 **O**; Letter 4 **OF**; Letter 5 **OF**; Letter 6 **O**; Letter 7 **O**; Letter 8 **O**

4 **a** *what's all the fuss; wishy-washy feelings, ridiculous fears, what rubbish!, stupid fears and anxieties.* Using this kind of language does not make an argument strong. It suggests that the writer does not have many facts or reasonable ideas to use, so has to resort to this kind of insult to people who might not agree.

b Letter 7; *weak, silly arguments*

c There is no right answer here, but if you find yourself convinced by Letter 2, read it again and think about the points made in the answer to **4a**. Be careful about thinking that people know what they are talking about because they sound certain, or they are clearly on one side or the other of an argument.

d There is no right answer here, but think about the points above, and about the Fact/Opinion balance in each letter. Note: opinion without fact is often appropriate as long as the opinion is logical.

25 Games — Part One Page 101

Preparing to read

1 There is no right answer because you are predicting. You could think it is Kirsty because she is leading the others, or Patricia because she seems to be trying to please the other girls, or Genevieve because she does not seem happy about being there.

2 The story is set in the country, it is about three girls on their way to somewhere from a railway station. One girl, Genevieve, seems unhappy with Kirsty, the leader of the trip, and the other, Patricia, seems like she wants to make up for Genevieve's anger and to please Kirsty.

Understanding the text

1 **a** False **b** True **c** True **d** False **e** True

2 **a** To Kirsty's Aunt Maude's big house in the country.

b She says the house had better be big if they are ever going to find it.

c Genevieve has long silky hair, smooth skin and nice eyes.

d She looks at you waiting for input.

e She does not give anything back.

f Because it means that she is not the outsider for a moment.

g Kirsty tries to impress Genevieve and looks up to her, but she feels superior to Patricia and looks down at her.

3 **a** contempt **b** akin **c** not letting well enough alone **d** inadequate **e** bellyaching **f** toffee-nosed **g** appeasement

4 **c** – the relationship between the three girls. Most of the text gives information about this. However, the text also achieves the other three purposes listed.

26 Games — Part Two Page 104

Preparing to read

b a description of the house.

Understanding the text

1 **a** True **b** True **c** True **d** False **e** True **f** True **g** False **h** True **i** False

2 **a** not loaded up **b** a kind of hanging bed **c** plant leaves **d** grown from seed **e** front of a building **f** made different **g** unhappily **h** stupid, ignorant **i** without interest **j** broken down and old **k** ruin and decay

3 c

Spotlight on language

Other examples of metaphor which suggest the house is alive: *come dourly to rest, seemed choked, hooded by verandas, gave the house a secretive air, like a suspicious face peering out from under a brimmed hat.*

27 Youth smoking drops and mobiles get credit — Page 108

Preparing to read

No right answers because this is a prediction, but the headline and sub-headline suggest the following.

a Youths are smoking less.

b Youths are using mobile phones more.

c Smoking and mobile phones may be related.

Understanding the text

1 **a** True **b** False **c** False **d** True **e** True **f** False **g** False **h** True

2 **a** Britain and Australia

b A slight decline in rate of 12 to 17 year olds smoking in the last week

c Mr Bates

d Action on smoking and health (UK)

e He thinks it has something to do with increasing mobile phone use amongst teenagers.

f NSW Health Department

g No; *figures had yet to be collated and confirmed*

h Smoking offers teenagers adult style, individuality, sociability, rebellion, peer-group bonding and adult aspiration

i Because they both provide the same things to teenagers.

j Because mobile phones are expensive (like cigarettes) so teenagers are likely to choose one or the other. They only need one to be 'cool'.

3 25%

4 One possible answer is that the Australian smoking experts would be reluctant to say anything until the theory is proved by research. It is also possible that because they have spent time and money providing smoking education, they might be reluctant to think that something else is the cause of any decrease in smoking rates. They might also be reluctant to think the solution could be as simple as something like the increase in mobile phone use. None of these is clear from the article.

28 Social comment — Page 112

Understanding the text

1 There is no single right answer here because cartoons are subjective – that is, one person may interpret a cartoon quite differently from another person. However, it seems likely that in Cartoon 1 the cartoonist is mainly making the following comments: **b**, **d** and **e**.

2 Here the cartoonist is likely to be mainly making the following comments: **c** and **f**. However he might also be making a minor comment about **b**, **d** and **e**.

3 **a** The changing scenery tells us that the young man has been on the bushwalk for a long time – long enough to pass through all the different kinds of scenery shown.

b It can take a long time to write a message but only a short time to read one.

c To show how far away the young man and young woman are; to show that the young man might as well have stayed in the city seeing he has seen nothing at all of the scenery; to show how mobiles are such a common part of everyday life – even used in cafes when you are with other people.

4 **a** He is enjoying himself but only through his mobile phone. He does not see any of the scenery.

b The characters are all relaxed and casual, and look like they are doing everyday normal things; the man has his hands in his coat pockets and is slouching; the boy has his hand in his pocket and has a casual stance also.

5 **a** He could have shown the actual words of the text message.

b This probably would not have been as effective as the simple, repetitive 'tap tap'.

6 **a** It makes you think the subject is vending machines.

b It keeps up the impression.

c This makes us focus on the action. It makes it clear that something is about to happen that will explain the whole cartoon. (It is like a short pause before the punchline of a joke.)

d The man's *Possibly* means that what he has seen is not so very surprising or shocking. Also his comment relates to the numbers of vending machines, not to the fact they now distribute guns. Both these things make the point that there is an acceptance of violence (represented by guns) in our society.

7 The youth in each cartoon could be said to be a stereotype – his cap is on backwards, his way of dress. The older people in the gun cartoon are stereotypically middle-aged — their glasses, their plain clothes. The young women in the cafe are stereotypes of young people about town with their mobile phones constantly in use.

It is your own opinion whether any of these stereotypes is harmful or insulting. In my view, however, they are just a technique to show quickly and clearly the social group the characters represent, and at the same time, to make the joke work.

29 The Gathering Page 116

Preparing to read

2 *Pre-* means 'before' or 'coming before'. The context of 'premonition' tells you that the word means 'a feeling that you get before something happens'. A premonition is usually a bad or negative feeling.

Understanding the text

1 **a** Three North **b** Cheshunt **c** Because they had been packed up and sent along with other things of his father's not sold at auction. **d** Because he always thought of his father as a serious man. **e** The windows and vents of the car were closed. **f** Looking at his dead father. **g** Both times he felt he was looking at something wrong and unnatural, something dead or bad that might come after him. **h** Nathaniel used to get chased by a monster, but now the monster was his dad.

2 **a**

3 **a** Heroes like Superman (who comes from the planet Krypton)

b Examples would be Donald Duck, Daffy Duck, Pluto

c A well-known geographical and nature magazine

4 **a** He is a serious boy, he is interested in the real world not a fantasy world, perhaps he is quite academic at school.

b His father has died or has disappeared for some reason. His father was well-off.

c His mother is a doctor or medical person of some kind.

d Nathaniel did not know his father, and/or had had little contact with him.

e Nathaniel has moved around and changed schools many times.

f She was not going to discuss it, the decision had been made.

g Nathaniel is somehow different from his mother. Perhaps he has supernatural powers or something similar.

h The memory was not pleasant. Perhaps something terrible or frightening had happened at the time of his dad's death or something terrible or frightening had caused his death.

5 It seems that Nathaniel and his mother have a tense, unhappy, distant relationship. It seems they don't communicate much at all. Nathaniel does not seem to feel much love towards his mother (at the moment anyway).

6 **a** field or piece of land used by everybody **b** blowing out in an unpleasant way (like a big burp) **c** shortened, not growing **d** felt the full strength of **e** nervous, jumpy **f** too interested in unpleasant things, especially death **g** looking at someone in an unpleasant way **h** smelling very badly

Spotlight on language

Writers often use the first person to make the story more immediate and vivid to the reader. Writing from the first person makes it seem like you are inside the person's head, and really hearing, seeing or feeling what *they* see, hear or feel.

30 The Lord of the Rings: The Two Towers Page 120

Preparing to read

3 The purpose of reviews is to both inform and entertain. Some reviewers might be more interested in being informative, while others might be more interested in being entertaining. All aim to be both to some extent, because otherwise people would not read their reviews. They are not aiming to persuade people to their point of view — although if they are really positive about a film, they would be pleased if people took their advice and went to see it.

Understanding the text

1 I think the reviewer would give at least 4 stars, probably 4 ½ or 5. She had very little to say that was negative, and overall was extremely enthusiastic about it.

2 **a**, **b**, **c**, **d**, **e**, **g**, **j**, **k**

3 **a** non-violent films, with good storylines and rich, complex characters.

b captivated

c making three movies at the same time

d Because you need to understand what happened before the action in this film; this film is really the middle of the story.

e hobbits, elves, goblins, dwarves, humans, the Night Riders and Orcs.

f The film *The Two Towers* does not begin with a summary of what happened in the first film *The Fellowship of the Ring.*

g Because of the battle scenes and the 'baddies' which will give them nightmares.

h It was difficult to understand the dialogue.

i No. The words *in this film anyway* tell the reader that the comments are only about *The Two Towers* not the series.

j Less true to the book

4 **a** one of the first **b** put aside all the negatives and gave it a try **c** a short summary **d** people (there is an implication that these people need pity because they did not see the first film) **e** just plain **f** destroys or eliminates **g** forcefulness, energy, excitement

5 **a** Amongst this strange world of non-human creatures it is easy to forget that there are humans as well.

b The reviewer is hinting that Gandalf might still be alive.

Responding to the text

1 This review's main purpose is to inform (there is a lot of factual information given). However, the reviewer is also aiming to entertain (there are a few jokes). And, because the reviewer is so positive about the film, it seems clear she wants to persuade the reader to go and see it as well.

31 The International Space Station Page 124

Preparing to read

These are the topics covered:

Milestones in space exploration; Countries involved in the space station; Dimensions of the space station; Benefits for humankind; Construction of the space station; Daily life on the space station

Understanding the text

1 **a**

2 **a** M **b** S **c** M **d** S **e** S **f** S **g** M **h** M **i** M **j** S

3 **a** In the past they were bitter enemies in the race to put a man on the moon.

b It is being constructed in space.

c It is a weightless environment (microgravity).

d We will be able to study the earth from a distance for as long as we need to.

e No, because there have been delays already.

f Because microgravity has a negative effect on muscles.

4 **a** important example of **b** combined effort **c** cooperation **d** never known or done before **e** possibilities **f** step backwards **g** waste away

5 **a** Yes, because some people think it is too risky or a waste of money when there are so many things that we could spend money on, on our own planet.

b For

c The writer writes about all the positive aspects of the ISS and generally seems to think that is an amazing achievement. If they did not think this, they would not list all the good things about it. Examples of language used are: *a new landmark achievement, a truly amazing aspect, an unprecedented opportunity, a step towards further space exploration, It will allow scientists to investigate, working hard for the benefit of us all.*

d The only negative point mentioned was the loss of lives in the Columbia disaster, and before that the Challenger disaster.

e You might think it is too much money to spend on such a thing when there are many problems to solve on this planet; you might think it is too risky — that any risk of loss of life means we should not do it; you might think it is a waste of time and money and lives because it may not lead to any significant benefit for us.

NOTES

NOTES